AF378692

Thompson and Peppercorn

-Locomotive Engineers

Thompson and Peppercorn
-Locomotive Engineers

Colonel H.C.B. Rogers, OBE

LONDON

IAN ALLAN LTD

First published 1979

ISBN 0 7110 0910 4

© Col H. C. B. Rogers 1979

Published by Ian Allan Ltd, Shepperton, Surrey;
and printed in the United Kingdom by
Ian Allan Printing Ltd

TO MY WIFE
whose first married home
lay beside the LNER

Below: Chief Mechanical Engineer and Staff in front of Class A2
Pacific locomotive No 525 *A. H. Peppercorn* at Doncaster on
31 December 1947. Back row, left to right: T. Little (Clerk), ?
(Technical Assistant), Goodchild (Clerk, one of Sir Nigel
Gresley's), W. Scott (Chief of Stores), J. Hillier (Technical
Assistant), Thom (Technical Assistant, son of Robert Thom), ?
(Technical Assistant); Front row, left to right: T. Windle (Chief
Draughtsman), H. Harper (Clerk, one of Sir Nigel Gresley's),
K. S. Robertson (Assistant to the Chief Mechanical Engineer),
Gosling (Chief Clerk), A. H. Peppercorn (Chief Mechanical
Engineer), J. F. Harrison (Assistant Chief Mechanical Engineer),
R. Hart-Davies (Technical Assistant), B. Spencer (Designer under
Sir Nigel Gresley). / *Crown Copyright/National Railway Museum,
York.*

Contents

Acknowledgements

For help in writing this book I am indebted above all to my friend J. F. Harrison, OBE, FIMechE, late Chief Engineer (Traction & Rolling Stock) British Railways, who has personally checked and commented on every chapter of this book, who has an unrivalled knowledge of LNER affairs and who was closely associated with the two persons who are the main subjects of this book. That great steam locomotive enthusiast, R. C. Bond, FICE, FIMechE, late CME British Railways and then Technical Adviser to the British Transport Commission, has been most helpful, not only in relation to his own experiences, but in introducing me to eminent personalities of the old LNER. My old friend R. A. Riddles, CBE, FIMechE, late Member for Mechanical & Electrical Engineering on the British Railways Executive, has as always been most willing to help with his own invaluable comments and advice, and I am indebted through him to C. Read late Mechanical Inspector on the LMS, for a most interesting report. No comment on LNER Pacifics could have been adequate without the wealth of information provided by Colonel K. R. M. Cameron, FIMechE, one time Motive Power Superintendent Scotland, and P. N. Townend, FIMechE, Traction Maintenance Engineer British Railways Eastern Region; and T. C. B. Miller, FIMechE, late Chief Engineer (Traction & Rolling Stock) British Railways has supplied me with his own experiences of Atlantics and Pacifics and North British 'Glens'. B. C.

Symes, CEng, MIMechE, late of the Doncaster Drawing Office, is invaluable in his information of happenings there during the Thompson regime. The reminiscences of C. G. Gold, FIMechE, late Mechanical Engineer Gorton, are a delight; and the record of his footplate experiences by K. H. Leech, late Chief Mechanical Engineer of the Westinghouse Brake & Signal Company, must be unique. My old friend André Chapelon, *Ingénieur en Chef Honoraire de la SNCF*, has helped me as usual with his penetrating comments and invaluable information. I am indebted to Mrs· Pat Mather for the attractive picture which emerges of her late husband A. H. Peppercorn, and Colonel W. H. Mather, OBE, TD, DL, has responded eagerly to my requests for assistance. R. F. Hanks, FIMechE, late Chairman of the Western Area Board of the British Transport Commission and Great Western enthusiast, has kindly come to my help in this primarily LNER book. K. J. Cook, OBE, FIMechE, late Mechanical Engineer first at Swindon then at Doncaster, has kindly given me his own reminiscences. Peter Grafton helped me considerably by the kindly gift of his own book on Edward Thompson. G. W. Carpenter, CEng, MIMechE, one of the comparatively few engineers still actively engaged with steam locomotives, has put me in touch with various sources of information and has lent me books and papers. Finally I must mention fellow members (who desire to remain anonymous) of the Railway Correspondence & Travel Society, who have so kindly placed at my disposal information gleaned in writing and editing the Society's histories of LNER locomotives.

1. The Background

It is important to remember that the job of a locomotive is to work trains of the weight and at the schedules required at the lowest possible cost, in terms of construction, consumption of fuel and water, and the time, materials, and labour of maintenance. Furthermore, these costs are those prevailing at the time the engine was built. If in later years, therefore, an engine is modified on account of increased costs under any one of the above heads, it does not necessarily reflect on the soundness of the original design. These facts appear to be self-evident, but they are perhaps lost sight of by enthusiasts, and even by locomotive engineers. It is unfortunate, indeed, that many of the old companies did not account the total costs of locomotive maintenance, and it was this omission which led to so many errors in comparing costs as between the locomotives of one pre-Grouping company and another. The LNER was not guilty of any such omission, but when Sir Nigel Gresley died in 1941, in the earlier stages of World War II, he left his successor with maintenance problems which did not exist when he designed the locomotives which he bequeathed.

As both the locomotive stock of the London & North Eastern Railway in 1941 and the designs which Edward Thompson formulated thereafter were influenced by classes owned by the pre-Grouping companies, it is necessary to go back before 1923 to understand locomotive policy in the latter days of the LNER.

The major companies which combined to form the London & North Eastern in 1923 were, of course, the North Eastern, which had practically a monopoly of the lines on the eastern side of England from south of York to the Scottish border, the Great Northern stretching from London to the industrial West Riding of Yorkshire, the Great Eastern serving practically the whole of East Anglia, the Great Central with its ramifications on the home ground about Manchester and Sheffield and a tentacle running south to London, the North British, mostly on the east side of Scotland, but with its Waverley route to Carlisle and its West Highland line to Fort William and Mallaig, and the Great North of Scotland which covered most of the north-east corner of the country. The locomotive stocks of these various companies had been designed, of course, to meet their own particular needs, and they had little in common either in tradition or appearance.

The then H. N. Gresley, who was chosen as the first Chief Mechnical Engineer of the London & North Eastern Railway, had occupied the same position on the Great Northern Railway since 1911. It could be anticipated, therefore, that the engines he would design for the new railway would be predominantly Great Northern both in their principal features and in their appearance. In fact, as a result of Gresley's appointment, the Great Northern 'look' of engines designed at Doncaster was retained consistently from Patrick Stirling's first 0-4-2 of 1867 to the Pacific designed under A. H. Peppercorn in 1948 — covering a far longer period than that of any other locomotive works in Great Britain, and probably in the world.

One small Doncaster feature is perhaps worth mentioning here — the flat 'S' curve of the footplate. This seems to have originated in the sweep over the driving wheels of Stirling's first 'eight-foot single', and appears in its final form on his later 2-4-0 engines. Ivatt's Atlantics have it, as, for example, do Gresley's 2-6-0s, 2-8-0s, and Pacifics. It does not appear on the 'Hunt' or 'Shire' 4-4-0s or on the J38 and J39 0-6-0s, for these were designed at Darlington and have the North Eastern single curve. Thompson's B1 4-6-0 also has this single curve, for an ex-Darlington man was responsible for the drawings.

However, before showing how Gresley met the locomotive needs of the LNER it is necessary to describe the principal locomotives available to the pre-Grouping companies, in order to determine what those needs were.

The Great Northern Railway

Both when H. A. Ivatt took over on the death of Patrick Stirling in 1895 and when H. N. Gresley succeeded Ivatt in 1911, the immediate need had been for more goods engines.

In 1874 Stirling introduced an 0-6-0 saddle tank class for local goods, with 4ft 7in coupled wheels and open cabs, which was immediately successful. In 1881 he built a considerable number of engines of the same type, but with smaller tanks and larger bunkers, which the LNER took over as Class J55. He built 10 more in 1892-93, but with closed cabs, which became Class J52 on the LNER; and another 15 appeared in 1896, after Ivatt had taken over. Ivatt continued the design, building another 52 from 1897 to 1899 and 40 more in 1901-08, but with certain modifications including a dome. In 1913 Gresley developed the class still further by building a side-tank version, primarily for use in shunting, which, in due course, was classified by the LNER as J51.

Similarly, 0-6-0 tender engines were derived from Stirling designs. Stirling took over from Archibald Sturrock in 1866 and produced his first 20 engines of this type in 1867-68. Between 1874 and 1881 he built another 36, with only slight modifications, and 72 more in 1886-89. This last lot were absorbed into LNER stock as J3. In 1896, after Ivatt has succeeded Stirling, 25 were added to this class; and still more were built in 1897-99, but this batch of 55 differed from Stirling's engines in having a dome. In 1899-1901 there followed 90 more, of which 12 went to the Midland & Great Northern Joint Railway. All these J3 class engines had 5ft 1in wheels.

In 1908 Ivatt built 15 0-6-0s of a new class with 5ft 8in wheels and a much bigger boiler for express goods and mixed traffic, which were classified J1 by the LNER. They were followed in 1909-10 by 20 0-6-0 engines with the normal 5ft 1in wheels but with a big boiler. Gresley built another 15 of these in 1911 but with superheaters. The LNER classified the saturated engines as J5 and the superheated as J6. In 1912 Gresley brought out another 10 of the express goods engines, but equipped them with superheaters. They became Class J2 and were used both on express goods trains and on certain passenger workings, including excursion trains.

By this time the 2-6-0 had proved its value as a mixed traffic engine on the Great Western Railway, and Gresley's next 5ft 8in engine for express goods and mixed traffic was a 2-6-0 with outside Walschaerts valve gear and 10in diameter piston valves. Ten of these were turned out from Doncaster, starting in 1912. They were satisfactory in service, but the boiler, of 4ft 8in diameter, was not quite big enough for the job. Accordingly, the next batch of 2-6-0s, which began to appear in 1914, had bigger boilers of 5ft 6in diameter, and, under the LNER, the earlier 10 engines were rebuilt with this bigger boiler. The LNER classifications were K1 and K2 respectively.

A still more powerful express goods engine being needed, Gresley produced in 1920 a remarkable 2-6-0 locomotive with a boiler 6ft in diameter, 5ft 8in wheels, and three cylinders with the middle valve operated by a conjugated gear. This engine, No 1000, was the first of a very numerous LNER Class K3. No 1000 was tried on express passenger trains, and it was on these trials that trouble was experienced with the valve gear — trouble that was to affect the design of all Gresley's Pacifics and which was to be partly responsible for the abandonment of the conjugated gear some 20 years later. No 1000 had piston valves of 8in diameter with a maximum travel of $6\frac{3}{8}$in at 75% cut-off. The conjugated gear was fitted in front of the cylinders and at high speed there was overtravel of the middle valve, with the result that the middle steam chest cover was struck and damaged by the valve spindle crosshead. For his first Pacifics, Gresley took the K3 valve gear, virtually unchanged, but he reduced the maximum valve travel to $4\frac{9}{16}$in by limiting the cut-off in full gear to 65%.

The Pacific was a logical development of Patrick Stirling's 4-2-2, the famous 'eight-foot single' of 1870. Ivatt built Atlantics as his principal main-line passenger engines, with 4-4-0s for the secondary services. The latter constituted a development of Stirling's 2-4-0 type, but with a leading bogie, and comprised two classes — the smaller (D3) built from 1896, and the larger (D2) from 1898, with a superheated version (D1) from 1910. The first of Ivatt's Atlantics (C2) was turned out from Doncaster in 1898, and, with its coupled wheels very close together, it was clearly derived from the Stirling 4-2-2. In 1902 a similar Atlantic, but with a much larger boiler of 5ft 6in diameter and a wide firebox made its impressive exit from Doncaster. The large Atlantics (C1) eventually numbered 91, and in their final superheated form they were amongst the most outstanding express passenger engines ever to run in the British Isles. Several of their brilliant performances have been recorded and are well known, but perhaps the most astonishing of all, when J. F. Harrison was on the footplate, has not previously appeared in print. He writes:[1]

'The date was a Saturday in 1925-26 when the "Scarborough Flyer" ran in two parts non-stop from Kings Cross to York. On this particular day the first part weighed 510 tons and was hauled by GN Atlantic No 3273, whereas the second part of 365 tons had a Pacific (A1 at that time), No 2543 I think. No 3273 took 17 minutes to pass Finsbury Park (usual time 6½-7 minutes) and in that short initial part of the run the exhaust injector failed and we were left with one cold water injector for the rest of the journey. From Finsbury Park to Chaloners Whin Junction (just short of York) the locomotive averaged 70.5mph! The Pacific running behind us by 10 minutes never saw us, much to the amusement of the Kings Cross driver, as No 3273 was driven by Molson of Doncaster Shed. During this journey every ounce of coal was used: ie about 7½ tons at about 50lb per mile. The main reason for the success of this engine was the Wootton-type wide firebox.'

T. C. B. Miller had experience of firing these Atlantics and told the author that they were comfortable engines — good riding, though very lively in an easy sort of way. He regarded them as excellent. There was a particular technique, he says, in their firing: as soon as the pressure dropped by 5lb, eight shovelfuls were put on, one in each corner and four down the middle.[2]

The Atlantics were the principal Great Northern express passenger engines up to the end of that company's separate existence; but in 1922 Gresley's first two Pacific locomotives were turned out from Doncaster. The boiler Gresley had taken from the K4 Pacifics of the Pennsylvania Railway, but though he also adopted their wide firebox he preferred the round top type to the K4's Belpaire. The Pacifics were designed to meet a requirement for the haulage of express trains up to 600 tons in weight. Initial trials with the first two having proved satisfactory, 10 more Pacifics were ordered, but these were not completed until after the Great Northern had been merged in the London & North Eastern.

Heavy mineral engines were first introduced on the GNR by Ivatt in 1901. They were 0-8-0s, and their unusual length for that time earned them the nickname of 'Long Toms'. Under the LNER they were classified Q2. In 1913 Gresley produced his own class of mineral engines. They also had eight coupled wheels, but, as with the 2-6-0s, he put a pony truck in front to make them 2-8-0s (Class O1). In 1918 he built a three-cylinder version, and this was in fact the first of Gresley's three-cylinder designs; it showed some advantage in starting over the two-cylinder 2-8-0s. The type of derived valve gear used for the inside cylinder was not entirely satisfactory, but in 1921 the first of a new class of three-cylinder 2-8-0s (LNER Class O2) was turned out from Doncaster, it differed from the 1918 engine in having the Gresley version of the conjugated valve gear designed by H. Holcroft, which was first fitted to 2-6-0 No 1000 and which was used for all subsequent three-cylinder engines designed during the Gresley regime.

The last class of Ivatt engines to be mentioned, as influencing LNER construction, were his 0-6-2 tanks of 1906 for suburban working (LNER Class N1). From these Gresley developed his superheated 0-6-2 tank engines of 1921, which became so well-known on London suburban traffic as the LNER Class N2.

The North Eastern Railway

On the North Eastern Railway locomotive development followed lines somewhat similar to those of the Great Northern, though the typical appearance of a North Eastern engine was not of such early origin. The locomotive lines which had become familiar at the time of the formation of the LNER dated from the advent of T. W. Worsdell as Locomotive Superintendent in 1885. His F class 4-4-0s of 1887 (LNER Class D22) heralded a steady development of express passenger engines which continued till 1922. Most of the F class were built as two-cylinder compounds, but these were all later converted to two-cylinder simples. In 1890 T. W. Worsdell was succeeded by his younger brother, Wilson Worsdell, who in 1892 produced his famous M class 4-4-0s (D17), which put up such astonishing performances in the 1895 races from London to Aberdeen. They were followed by the very similar Q class (also designated D17 by the LNER), and the two Q1 4-4-0s which were built specifically for racing, should the contest be resumed, and which had coupled wheels of no less than 7ft 7½in diameter. Wilson Worsdell's R class (D20) engines of 1899 were amongst the best 4-4-0s to run in Great Britain. They had 8¾in diameter piston valves and large steam and exhaust ports; by 1907 60 had been built and they were handling the bulk of the East Coast traffic. The R class engines regularly worked the 12.20pm Newcastle to Sheffield express, which before World War I was the fastest train in the British Empire. In 1908 the first engines were built at Darlington Works, and these, appropriately, were the big and impressive R1 class 4-4-0s with a boiler of 5ft 6in diameter and a large grate area of

27sq ft. There were 10 in the class and under LNER ownership they became D21. They were successful engines, probably better than Wilson Worsdell's Atlantics, for in 1910 they handled most of the Scotch expresses. Nevertheless, though able to pull much heavier loads, they never seemed to have the sparkle of the earlier R class and they had a reputation of being coal-eaters.

Wilson Worsdell was a pioneer in England of the 4-6-0 engine. His S class (B13) of 1899 had 6ft coupled wheels and were used mostly for express goods traffic. Ten were built in 1899-1900 and 10 more in 1906. The S1 class (B14), of which five were built in 1900, were very handsome engines with 6ft 8½in coupled wheels and were intended for the heavy East Coast expresses.

The next 4-6-0 locomotives were Sir Vincent Raven's S2 class (B15) of 1911-13 with 6ft coupled wheels, of which 20 were built for mixed traffic, particularly fast freight. But Raven's most notable 4-6-0s were his three-cylinder S3 class (B16) with 5ft 8in coupled wheels for express freight trains. The first batch of 50 engines was completed in 1919-20 and another 20 were turned out in 1923, after the formation of the LNER. The S3s were perhaps the best of Raven's engines.

Wilson Worsdell followed Ivatt very quickly in building large Atlantics. The first of his V class (C6) came out in 1903, a year after No 251 of the Great Northern, and also with a 5ft 6in diameter boiler. Gateshead Works built 10 in 1903-04, and another 10, with some minor modifications, came from Darlington Works in 1910. They did the work for which they had been designed, but were by no means outstanding. Two much better Atlantics were designed by W. M. Smith, Chief Draughtsman at Gateshead, and built in 1906. They were four-cylinder compounds on Smith's system and were perhaps the best express engines ever to run on the North Eastern. Unfortunately Smith died before they were completed or there would probably have been more of them. (The North Eastern wanted 10 more but the executors of Smith's estate demanded too much money for the use of his patents.)

In 1911 Raven began the production of his own Atlantics of Class Z (C7), three-cylinder engines with three sets of Stephenson's valve gear, all inside. Construction continued in 1914-18 and there were eventually 50 of them. The Z Atlantics were fine engines and were very popular with their drivers, and, though they could roll on occasions, their riding was very comfortable.

Like Gresley, Raven built two Pacific type locomotives in 1922, and three more followed in 1924. They were virtually a 'stretched' version of the Z class Atlantics, with the same arrangement of three cylinders, all driving on the leading coupled axle and with three sets of inside Stephenson's valve gear. They were disappointing engines. The boiler steamed well, but the front end design was poor, particularly in respect of steam passages and valve gear. However, they bequeathed a legacy to the future, for the drive on the leading coupled axle influenced Thompson in the design of his Pacifics.[3]

T. W. Worsdell's standard goods engines were the C class (J21) 0-6-0s, construction of which was started in 1886 and continued up till 1895 (latterly, of course, under Wilson Worsdell), when there was a total of 201. Most of them were originally two-cylinder compounds, but all were converted in due course to simple expansion. Before the last of the C class had been built, Wilson Worsdell was turning out the first of his very similar P class (J24), and the rather larger P1s followed from 1898. In 1905 came the P2 class (J26) with a much bigger boiler of 5ft 6in diameter. A modified and heavier version, the P3 class (J27), was built from 1906. Of Wilson Worsdell's 0-6-0s, there were 70 Class Ps, 140 P1s, 50 P2s, and 115 P3s.

The first of the North Eastern 0-8-0 mineral engines were built in 1901, the same year as those of the Great Northern, but Wilson Worsdell's T class had outside cylinders. The T class had piston valves, but at this period some trouble was still being experienced with them and the succeeding T1s, though generally similar, had slide valves. In 1913 Raven built the T2 class, which did not differ much from the earlier 0-8-0s, but were superheated. In 1919 Raven produced his T3 class of three-cylinder 0-8-0s. All these North Eastern eight-coupled mineral engines were very successful. The LNER classified both Wilson Worsdell's classes as Q5, Raven's two-cylinder engines as Q6, and his three-cylinder ones as Q7. Raven, it will be noticed, did not follow Gresley in adopting a leading pony truck.

The other North Eastern engines which merit a mention are the three-cylinder D class (LNER H1) 4-4-4 passenger tanks built in 1913, and the Y class (A7) three-cylinder 4-6-2 mineral tanks of 1910, intended for the shorter coal train workings from collieries to ports.

The Great Eastern Railway

The locomotive traditions of the Great Eastern's latter years started at the same time as that of the North Eastern; for James Holden succeeded T. W. Worsdell on the latter's departure to Gateshead in 1885, and his influence is clear on every subsequent Great Eastern engine. Holden was a Great Western man, and as Carriage Works Manager at Swindon he had been G. J. Churchward's immediate chief. He was the first locomotive engineer to go in for a really considerable degree of standardisation. Boilers, cylinders, axles, axleboxes, motion, and other components were the same for his 2-2-2 and 2-4-0 express engines (these two classes being identical except for the wheel arrangement), his 2-4-0 mixed traffic engines, his goods 0-6-0s, and his 2-4-2 tanks; all of which were built from 1886 onwards.[4] Holden's standardisation policy influenced Edward Thompson, who had a great weakness for Stratford and its ideas.[5] Holden's earlier engines had a stovepipe chimney, but his later designs from 1898 onwards had a brass-capped lipped chimney of very Swindon appearance.

Of all Holden's locomotives, the most outstanding, and indeed the most famous, was his 'Claud Hamilton' class 4-4-0s, of which the first, No 1900 *Claud Hamilton*, was turned out from Stratford Works in 1900. It was an extremely handsome engine, painted in the Great Eastern royal blue livery with vermilion coupling rods, scarlet lining, brass embellishments (including the chimney cap) and the Great Eastern armorial device on the driving splashers. Edward Thompson admired this livery so much that he adopted the royal blue with red lining for his rebuild of No 4470 *Great Northern*.[6] Ten more 'Clauds' were built in 1900, and further batches of 10 were turned out in 1901, 1902, and 1903, incorporating various minor modifications. All of these had round-top fireboxes, but a batch of 1904 were given Belpaire fireboxes and this feature was retained in all the subsequent batches, which appeared every year from 1906 to 1911. Belpaire fireboxes were in due course fitted to the earlier engines, and all the 'Clauds' were eventually superheated. In 1922 A. J. Hill rebuilt one of them with a new boiler of 5ft diameter instead of the original 4ft 9in. This became the prototype of 10 more 'Claud Hamiltons' which emerged from Stratford in 1923. These were painted in the LNER green livery, but two of them were given brass chimney caps and were used on all Royal train workings. These 10 engines were later fitted with an extended smokebox carried on a saddle. The 'Clauds' were classified D15 by the LNER, with the exception of these last 10 'Super - Clauds', which became D16. Under the LNER a number of D15s were rebuilt as D16, and by 1932, 30 had been so converted.

In 1912 A. J. Hill became Locomotive Superintendent, and in the same year he produced his excellent 1500, or S69, class 4-6-0s (LNER B12). These very good looking engines, with the same lines and livery as the 'Claud Hamiltons', were intended to meet the need for express engines with a higher tractive effort and a greater adhesion than the 4-4-0s, but without exceeding the limited axle loads allowed on the Great Eastern permanent way. This was a remarkably successful design, and when construction ceased in 1921 there were 70 engines in the class.

Some of the most remarkable of Great Eastern locomotives were the little 0-6-0 tank engines designed by Holden in 1886, which were still handling the bulk of the Great Eastern's very intensive suburban service up till the end of its independent existence.

Hill introduced the very fine 1000 class of superheated 0-6-2 tank engines with 4ft 10in coupled wheels in 1915, to take over suburban working from Holden's little engines. Only two were built in that year, but more appeared between 1921 and 1924. The LNER liked them so much that they were designated as a standard for the Great Eastern section, and 112 more were built between 1925 and 1928, though with round-top instead of Belpaire fireboxes. The LNER classified them as N7.

Development of James Holden's 0-6-0 goods engines was continued by Hill, who in 1912 produced the first superheated version, the 1240 class (J18). In 1916 the very similar 1140 class (J19) appeared. In 1920 came Hill's last 0-6-0 design, the 1270 class (J20), which had the 1500 class 4-6-0 boiler and were the biggest and most powerful 0-6-0 engines (with the possible exception of Bulleid's ugly engines for the Southern) ever to run in Great Britain. All these Hill engines had Belpaire fireboxes.

The Great Central Railway

The Great Central Railway was in some respects unique. It only acquired its title in 1897, after the provincial Manchester, Sheffield & Lincolnshire Railway had built a new trunk line southwards to London; and it had virtually only one Chief Mechanical Engineer for the whole of its existence, because J. G. Robinson was appointed in 1900 and held office until the Grouping. Robinson came from the Waterford, Limerick & Western Railway of Ireland (later part of the Great Southern & Western), and brought with him the chimney he had used on the Irish railway. He had pronounced views on chimneys and once said that 'a chimney to a locomotive is like a hat to a man; the finishing touch.'[7] Robinson was a great administrator who provided the Great Central with a fine fleet of locomotives to meet its traffic needs. He decided the types of locomotive that he wanted but, like many chief mechanical engineers, he was not himself a designer, and it was common knowledge at Gorton that the locomotives were actually designed by W. Rowland, the Chief Locomotive Draughtsman.[8] Some of Rowland's work was outstanding, but the bigger engines were spoiled by his extraordinary insistence that the grate area should not exceed 26sq ft; for whilst this was adequate for engines of moderate dimensions, it was far too little for the big-boilered 4-6-0s.

The traditional and elegant outline of all Great Central engines may be said to have started with a single 4-4-0 designed and built by Messrs Kitson & Co for the MS&LR to exhibit at the 1887 Jubilee Exhibition in Manchester. (It is an odd coincidence that Kitson built three 4-4-0s with very similar lines for the Waterford, Limerick & Western in 1896 — one of which was No 53 *Jubilee* — during Robinson's Locomotive Superintendency.) The type was finalised in the Class 11 4-4-0s of 1895 with Belpaire fireboxes, which became a standard fitting for all Great Central locomotives.

Robinson's first locomotives were the 9J class (J11) 0-6-0 goods engines of 1901, of which 174 were built up to 1910. They were very capable and popular, as is evident from their absurd nickname of 'Pom-Poms'. The first express passenger locomotives of his regime were the 1013, or 11B, Class (D9) 4-4-0s of 1902, of which 40 were built during the following two years. Construction of 89 outside cylinder 0-8-0 mineral engines of the 1052, or 8A, class (Q4) also started in 1902 and was continued till 1911. A further class of 1902 (Class 8, and LNER B5) consisted of 14 4-6-0 mixed traffic engines with 6ft 1in coupled wheels which were intended for fast freight. They so often worked the express fish trains from Grimsby that they were popularly known as the 'Fish Engines'. In 1903-05 40 Class 9K (C13) 4-4-2 tank engines were built for suburban services, and these were followed in 1907 by 12 of a slightly heavier version, designated 9L (C14). These engines were very similar to four 4-4-2 tanks built by Kitson for the Waterford, Limerick & Western in 1896-97.

Main-line passenger services soon needed a more powerful engine, and Robinson was not certain whether this should be an Atlantic or a 4-6-0. He decided, therefore, to try both before making up his mind, and two of each were built in 1903 — the 4-6-0s being convertible to Atlantics. Apart from their wheel arrangement the engines, as in Churchward's trial on the Great Western, were identical. But unlike Churchward, Robinson preferred the Atlantics and ordered another 25 of this 192, or 8B, class (C4). To compare compound with simple expansion, five three-cylinder compound Atlantics (C5) were built in 1905-06 on Smith's system. However, no more compounds were built, so Robinson presumably came to the conclusion that they offered no particular advantage. The two 4-6-0s were classified 8C. Under the LNER they became B1, but, on the construction of Edward Thompson's 4-6-0s, the latter engines were classified B1 and the GC 4-6-0s were altered to B18. Robinson liked these two engines and in 1906 built 10 more, but, in order to make them more suitable for fast perishable goods trains as well as express passenger, he had them fitted with 6ft 7in coupled wheels instead of the 6ft 9in of the 8Cs. The 10 of 1906 were officially the 8F class, but they were always known as the 'Imminghams' because the first of the class was named *Immingham*. The LNER called them Class B4. Also in 1906 there were 10 4-6-0s with 5ft 3in coupled wheels for fast goods trains of the 1105, or 8G, class (B9).

As new and heavy London suburban trains required something more powerful than the 4-4-2 tanks, the 9N class (A5) inside-cylinder 4-6-2 tank engines were built from 1911 onwards. There were eventually 31, the last being completed in 1923. The first of a new series of eight-coupled mineral engines was also turned out in 1911; but these, Class 8K (O4), were 2-8-0s. Many engineers believe them to be the best of all Robinson's engines. The design was adopted as a standard in World War I and they were used in World War II as well, 91 being sent out to the Middle East in 1941.

The impressive and good-looking 'Sir Sam Fay', or No 1, class (B19) of six engines appeared in 1912-13, to work heavy express passenger trains, and in 1913-14 there was a mixed traffic version, the 'Glenalmond', or 1A, class (B8) with 5ft 7in coupled wheels. These engines were 4-6-0s with two inside cylinders, 10in diameter piston valves, and a large boiler of 5ft 6in diameter. But the 26sq ft grate area was too small and their performance was not brilliant.

The 'Director', or 11E, class (D10) 4-4-0s were turned out in 1913, and these 10 engines could do the same work as the Atlantics on a lower coal consumption. Eleven more were built from 1919 with larger cabs and certain other modifications, and these were known as the 'Improved Directors' or 11F class (D11). The 'Directors' of both series were the best express engines that the Great Central ever had.

Between 1914 and 1917 20 large 1B class (L3) 2-6-4 mineral tank engines with 5ft 1in coupled wheels were built to work coal traffic between the North Nottinghamshire coal fields and the Immingham and Grimsby docks.

Robinson's largest express passenger engines were the six four-cylinder 4-6-0s of the 'Lord Faringdon', or 9P class (B3) with the same boiler as the 'Sir Sam Fays'. These also suffered from the inadequate grate area and were heavy coal burners. At the time of their construction R. A. Thom was Works Manager at Gorton and he told a story to J. F. Harrison which shows that Robinson, great man though he was, took no part in the detail of locomotive design. When the first of the 'Lord Faringdons' was put in steam outside the erecting shop and moved up and down, the CME watched the movement of the engine. Afterwards he turned to Thom and said: 'I thought I had said that this locomotive was to have four cylinders, not two, as appears the case, because it exhausts four times per revolution, whereas it should exhaust eight times.' Thom then drew a diagram in chalk on a plate outside the erecting shop to show how with the setting of the cranks on these engines the back port of cylinder 2 exhausted coincidentally with the front port of cylinder 1, and so on.[9]

A mixed traffic version of the 'Lord Faringdons' with 5ft 8in coupled wheels appeared in 1921, which was known as the 9Q class (B7), and was the last Great Central design. They were intended primarily for the heavy express fish trains from Grimsby to London, and no less than 38 were built. They consumed coal in such enormous quantities that they acquired the expressive nickname of 'Black Pigs'.

Meanwhile there had been some peculiar construction in 1918. Some 2-8-0s were fitted with a larger boiler of 5ft 6in diameter, Class 8M, and three 4-6-0s were built with 5ft 8in coupled wheels, classified 8N (B6), which were identical with the large boiler 2-8-0s except for their wheel arrangement. Neither class was conspicuously successful because the grate area remained at 26sq ft. The reason for the construction of the 4-6-0s is something of a mystery, because there was no major improvement in design over the already existing 'Glenalmonds'.

The North British Railway

It was for the North British Railway that Dugald Drummond designed the first engines with his characteristic outline and smokebox wing plates, which were subsequently to be seen in large numbers on the Caledonian, Highland, Glasgow & South Western, and London & South Western Railways. Drummond repeated the type when he left the North British for the Caledonian and then took it with him to the London & South Western. His brother introduced it on the Highland and the Glasgow & South Western. On the North British it was continued by Holmes and Reid to the end of that railway's separate existence, and Lambie and McIntosh stuck to it on the Caledonian. There were few rivals in appearance to this classic Drummond locomotive.

The ancestors of the Drummond 'family' were his 12 'Abbotsford' 4-4-0s with 6ft 6in coupled wheels of 1877-79, built to work the through Midland Scotch expresses from St Pancras over the Waverley route from Carlisle to Edinburgh. They were rebuilt in 1902 and 1904 and, as there was a slight difference in weight between the two rebuildings, the LNER classified them D27 and D28 respectively. Between 1884 and 1899 Matthew Holmes (who succeeded Drummond in 1881) continued the same general type with three very similar classes of 6ft 6in 4-4-0s, which were assimilated into one class D31 by the

LNER. They were very successful engines and in 1895 they worked the racing trains between Edinburgh and Aberdeen. Forty-eight of them passed into LNER ownership. In 1886-88 Holmes built 12 4-4-0s with 7ft coupled wheels (D25) which were intended to operate the Aberdeen services when the Tay Bridge was reopened in 1887, and they were subsequently used on Aberdeen expresses from both Edinburgh and Glasgow. Holmes's last express locomotives were built in 1903 (D26). They had 6ft 6in coupled wheels and took over the working of the heaviest express trains on both the Aberdeen and Carlisle routes. For the West Highland Railway Holmes designed a class of mixed traffic 4-4-0s with 5ft 7in coupled wheels (D35), and these were built from 1894 to 1896. They did most of the work on the West Highland from its opening, but they were not as good as the remainder of Holmes's 4-4-0s, and the enginemen disliked them on account of their lack of adhesion, which told badly on the curves and gradients of the West Highland. They had all gone a year after Grouping.

W. P. Reid succeeded Holmes in 1904. His first 4-4-0s were 12 excellent 'Intermediates' of 1906-07 (D32) with 6ft coupled wheels for mixed traffic working, and intended principally for the fast fish trains from Mallaig and Aberdeen and the meat trains. They were very successful on both these and passenger trains, and all Reid's subsequent 4-4-0s differed from them only in detail.

Reid's first express passenger locomotives, however, were not 4-4-0s, but some big Atlantics which were perhaps the most impressive looking engines ever to run in Scotland before the Grouping. Fourteen were built in 1906, six in 1911, and a final two in 1921. They were intended for working the difficult Waverley and Aberdeen routes. The choice of a 4-4-2 rather than a 4-6-0 seems surprising, but Reid may have thought it important to have a flexible wheelbase for the numerous curves, at the sacrifice of some adhesion. They were powerful engines, but heavy on coal consumption. T. C. B. Miller says that they were spoken of with high regard by the drivers, but he is not sure that the firemen loved them so well. 'But of course', he adds, 'they were tremendous work horses.'[10]

In 1909-11 Reid built a batch of 6ft 6in 4-4-0s which were developed from his 1906 'Intermediates'. They were given names from the stories of Sir Walter Scott and were known as the 'Scott' class (D29). They worked express passenger trains on all the important North British lines. At the same time a mixed traffic version with 6ft coupled wheels (D33) was introduced, and these only differed from the 'Scotts' in wheel diameter. Several of them were allotted to the West Highland. In 1912-20 more 'Scotts' were built, but these were superheated (D30). Under the LNER all the saturated 'Scotts' were superheated and joined Class D30.

Reid's best and most famous engines were the 6ft 'Superheated Intermediates' of 1913-20. There were 32 on the class (D34) and as they were all named after glens they became known as the 'Glen' class. T. C. B. Miller knew them well and says 'they were in my opinion the best engines the NB had — tough, good steaming, sure-footed, and reliable. They did magnificent work on the West Highland, where reliability mattered a great deal.'[11] They took over practically all the traffic on the West Highland, and several of them were still working on that line when the LNER was merged in British Railways. The maximum load for a 'Glen' on the West Highland was 190 tons, so that as the heavier rolling stock made its appearance on the through trains to Fort William, some double-heading with two 'Glens' became necessary. Nevertheless, none of the more powerful engines which were brought in to replace the 'Glens' stood up as well as they did to the heavy pounding over the steep gradients and awkward curves of this difficult route.[12]

NBR goods engines were all 0-6-0s with 5ft wheels. There were three classes: Holmes's engines of 1888-1900 which were all rebuilt by Reid (J36), Reid's first class of 1906-13 (J35), and Reid's second class of 1914-21 (J37). The most notable tank engines were two classes of 4-4-2Ts built in 1911-13 (C15) and 1915-21 (C16), primarily to work the coast services running in connection with the Clyde steamers, and the Balloch trains serving the Loch Lomond steamers.

The Great North of Scotland Railway

The Great North of Scotland Railway was unique in that all its traffic was worked by 4-4-0 tender engines. Some of those which came into LNER ownership were very old. The most modern were engines with 6ft 1in coupled wheels, grouped in two classes — one of 32 built between 1893 and 1898 (D41) and the other of 21 built between 1899 and 1921 (D40). Always a poverty-stricken line, the GNSR was in need of more modern and suitable locomotives. (Poverty-stricken as it was, however, it had carriages built of solid walnut! When these carriages were scrapped a number of beautiful desks were made out of the walnut; J. F. Harrison had one at Cowlairs.)[13]

Summary of Pre-Grouping Locomotives

Apart from the new Pacifics, which had hardly as yet made any impact on the passenger train working, the best express passenger locomotives were undoubtedly the Great Northern Atlantics. The North Eastern Z class Atlantics, the Great Eastern 4-6-0s and 'Claud Hamilton' 4-4-0s, and the Great Central 'Directors' were very good and on top of their respective jobs. On the North British the Atlantics, 'Scotts' and 'Glens' were all good, but the traffic was beginning to get beyond their capabilities.

In mixed traffic the Great Northern led easily with its 1000 class 2-6-0s, and the larger boilered two-cylinder class were useful engines. The North Eastern, however, had some very good mixed traffic engines in the S3 4-6-0s. There were three notable classes of heavy freight locomotives — the Great Northern three-cylinder 2-8-0s, the Great Central two-cylinder 2-8-0s, and the North Eastern three-cylinder 0-8-0s. Of the 0-6-0 goods engines, the Great Northern J6s, the Great Eastern 1270 class, the Great Central 'Pom-Poms', and the North Eastern P3s merit special mention. The best passenger tank engines were probably the Great Northern and Great Eastern 0-6-2s, the Great Central 4-6-2s, the North Eastern 4-4-4s, and the North British 4-4-2s.

It will be observed that, even apart from its Pacifics, the Great Northern made the most advanced contribution to the common locomotive stock. Indeed, if Gresley could not yet match the magnificent stud of locomotives which G. J. Churchward of the Great Western had handed over to his successor, he had at least put the Great Northern ahead of every other British railway in locomotive design.

The stage is now set for the appearance of the two locomotive engineers who are the subject of this book, of whom one hated Gresley and the other was devoted to him — Edward Thompson and Arthur Peppercorn.

Notes

1 J. F. Harrison, letter to the author
2 T. C. B. Miller, information to the author
3 Harrison, op cit
4 W. F. Pettigrew; *A Manual of Locomotive Engineering*; Charles Griffin & Co, 2nd edn revised, 1901, pp36-39
5 Harrison, op cit
6 ibid
7 George Dow; *Great Central*; Ian Allan Ltd, vol III, 1965, p124
8 Harrison, op cit
9 ibid
10 T. C. B. Miller, letter to the author
11 ibid
12 The Railway Correspondence & Travel Society, *Locomotives of the LNER* Part 4, p46
13 Harrison, op cit

Above right: LNER Class K3 2-6-0, built in 1924. / *LPC*

Right: No 251, the first GN large boiler Atlantic, built 1902. / *LPC*

Top left: A typical Atlantic duty in LNER days; No 4433 on the 'West Riding Pullman'. / *E. R. Wethersett*

Centre left: Gresley's first Pacific: A1 class No 1470, built 1922. / *LPC*

Below: An A1 class Pacific in LNER livery; No 1476 (later No 4476 *Royal Lancer*). / *H. Gordon Tidey*

Right: An O2 in BR days: No 63985 at Beeston, Leeds. / *Eric Treacy*

Below right: NER R class 4-4-0, built 1899 (later LNER Class D20). / *LPC*

63985

2011
NORTH   EASTERN

Left: LNER Class D21 (ex-NER R1 class) No 1244. / *H. Gordon Tidey*

Below: NER S3 class 4-6-0 No 846, built 1919. / *LPC*

Right: Two B16s, No 61422 and 61421, on the 9.20am Newcastle to Holloway train at Otterington in 1952. / *J. W. Hague*

Below right: LNER Class C7 Atlantic (ex-NER Class Z) No 2197 leaving Harrogate on the 'Queen of Scots' Pullman express. / *Ian Allan Library*

Top: LNER Class C9 Atlantic (ex-NER Class Z) rebuilt with a booster under cab and tender. / *LPC*

Above: North Eastern Pacific No 2401 *City of Kingston-upon-Hull* in LNER colours. / *LPC*

Left: LNER Class A2 Pacific (ex-NER) leaving York. / *H. Gordon Tidey*

Above right: LNER Class J27 (ex-NER Class P3) 0-6-0, as BR No 65855 with a coal train in August 1963. / *P. Robinson*

Right: GER 'Claud Hamilton' class 4-4-0 No 1831 with Belpaire firebox (LNER Class D15). / *LPC*

Above: 'Claud Hamilton' class LNER
D16/2, or 'Super-Claud', with
larger boiler. / *Ian Allan Library*

Right: LNER Class D16/2 'Super-
Claud' with an extended smokebox.
No 8783 was one of the Royal
engines with a brass chimney cap.
/ *Ian Allan Library*

Below right: LNER Class D16/3: a
'Super-Claud' rebuilt with a round-top
firebox, but retaining its large boiler
and also the decorative footplating.
/ *R. E. Vincent*

Far right, top: B12 4-6-0 leaving
Kittybrewster on the old Great North
of Scotland main line. Engine fitted
with round-top firebox.
/ *P. Ransome-Wallis*

Far right, bottom: 'Pom-Pom'
No 1116 on a Sheffield to
Cleethorpes excursion train in July
1919. / *P. Ransome-Wallis*

Above left: LNER Class O4 2-8-0 (ex-GCR) on a coal train from the South Yorkshire coalfields in the BR era. / *J. B. Welldon*

Left: A Great Central 'Director' on an express train. / *LPC*

Above: LNER Class B3 (ex-GCR 'Lord Faringdon' class) 4-6-0 No 6166 *Earl Haig* on a Manchester to Marylebone express in 1927. / *P. Ransome-Wallis*

Centre right: NBR Atlantic No 874 *Dunedin* (LNER Class C11), Edinburgh. / *LPC*

Bottom right: LNER Class D34 (ex-NBR 'Glen') 4-4-0 No 9493 *Glen Luss*, with smokebox wing plates removed. / *LPC*

Right: 'Glen' class 4-4-0s (LNER D34), BR Nos 62496 *Glen Loy* and 62471 *Glen Falloch*, on a Fort William to Glasgow train about half a mile south of Ardlui.
/ *W. J. V. Anderson*

Below: GNSR 4-4-0 No 49 *Gordon Highlander* (LNER Class D40).
/ *G. W. Morrison*

Bottom: LNER Class D40 (ex-GNSR) 4-4-0, BR No 62264, entering Boat of Garten with a local train from Craigellachie. / *G. L. Wilson*

2. Thompson and Peppercorn: Pre-Grouping Years

It is curious that four out of the five last locomotive chiefs of the Great Northern and London & North Eastern Railways were sons of clergymen. Patrick Stirling's father was the Reverend Robert Stirling, a Minister of the Church of Scotland; Henry Alfred Ivatt was the son of the Rector of Coveney; Herbert Nigel Gresley was the fifth child of the Reverend Nigel Gresley, Rector of Netherseale; and Arthur Henry Peppercorn was one of the eleven children of the Reverend Alfred Thomas Peppercorn, Rector of Stoke Prior. The odd one out was Edward Thompson, for his father, Francis Edward Thompson, was an assistant master, and later Governor, of Marlborough College. Even he had clerical connections, for Marlborough was founded as a school for the sons of clergy and has maintained that connection ever since. It was a tradition which would have pleased that devout Methodist preacher Timothy Hackworth of the Stockton & Darlington Railway, the first Locomotive Superintendent in history.

Francis Thompson had four children, of which the three elder were girls and the youngest a son. He was a Greek scholar of some distinction, and he seems to have bequeathed some of his tastes in education and learning to his son Edward. In 1889, when he was eight years old, Edward was sent off to a preparatory school in Reigate, St David's. There, in due course, he passed the Common Entrance examination and in 1894 returned to Marlborough as a pupil. A much senior boy had either recently left, or was about to leave, Marlborough to continue his education as a pupil at the Crewe Works of the London & North Western Railway; it is possible, but perhaps unlikely, that a chance encounter with this boy, Nigel Gresley, founded Edward Thompson's eventual antipathy to his future chief.

In 1899 Thompson left Marlborough in his turn, but he went to Pembroke College, Cambridge, where he read Mechanical Sciences. He was there till 1902, when he obtained a Class 3 degree in the final examinations of the Mechanical Sciences Tripos. Gresley had gone to the new Horwich Works of the Lancashire & Yorkshire Railway in 1898 to study locomotive design. In 1900 he was appointed Outdoor Assistant to the Lancashire & Yorkshire Railway Carriage and Wagon Superintendent, and in the following year he was posted to the L&Y Carriage & Wagon Works at Newton Heath, near Manchester, as Assistant Works Manager. He was still there when Thompson joined Beyer Peacock & Company at Manchester as a pupil in the drawing office[1], though whether the two Old Marlburians ever met at this stage is unknown.

The third of this trio of future LNER CMEs, Arthur Henry Peppercorn, was born in 1889 at the village of Stoke Prior, half way between Birmingham and Worcester. He was privately educated at first, and then in 1901 he went to Hereford Cathedral School, a minor public school with a considerable reputation. His father hoped that his son would follow him into the Church. With this in mind, he asked young Arthur what career he would like to adopt, and was considerably annoyed when his son replied firmly that he intended to be an engine driver. However, there was no turning the boy from his love of steam locomotives, and in 1905 he left Hereford Cathedral School to enter the Doncaster Locomotive Works of the Great Northern Railway as a premium apprentice under H. A. Ivatt. A fellow apprentice was W. O. Bentley, the famous originator of Bentley cars, who became a great friend. Gresley had been promoted Assistant Superintendent of the L&Y Carriage & Wagon Department in

1904, and in 1905 he was appointed Superintendent of the Great Northern Railway Carriage & Wagon Department. He thus arrived at Doncaster at about the same time as Peppercorn. Gresley took a great liking to the young apprentice. He was always sending for him. Arthur got to know the Gresley boys and girls very well and was treated as one of the family.[2]

Thompson left Beyer Peacock in 1904 and joined the Midland Railway at Derby, where he gained experience in various departments of the Locomotive Works and worked as an improver in Derby sheds. In 1905 he left the Midland and went to Woolwich Arsenal. In 1906 he joined the North Eastern Railway and was posted to Hull Dairycoates as assistant to the District Locomotive Superintendent. In 1909 he was transferred to Gateshead and appointed assistant to the Northern Running Superintendent. Wilson Worsdell was at that time CME of the North Eastern Railway, but the next year he was succeeded by his Assistant, Vincent Raven. Very soon after becoming CME, Raven visited the United States to study electrification on American railways. Edward Thompson was one of the party selected to accompany him.[3]

In 1911, as stated in the last chapter, Gresley became CME of the Great Northern Railway. In his new capacity he continued to make much use of Peppercorn, who was devoted to him. Gresley had already marked him out for promotion owing to his outstanding ability, and he was very soon given his first appointment as assistant to the District Locomotive Inspector at Ardsley. At about the same time, in 1912, Edward Thompson was appointed to the post vacated by Gresley, as Carriage & Wagon Superintendent at Doncaster, with, of course, Gresley as his immediate chief. It was an important post for a young man of 31, and he must have been strongly recommended by Raven. (Gresley had become Carriage & Wagon Superintendent at about the same age and was remarkably young to be a CME.) In 1913 Thompson married Raven's younger daughter, Guendolen. On the face of it, this was a fortunate liaison for an ambitious young railway engineer, but the marriage

seems to have become subjected to certain strains between the pair.

Before the outbreak of World War I, Peppercorn was transferred to the similar, but more important, post of assistant to the district Locomotive Superintendent at Peterborough. In May 1915 Raven was given a Government appointment as Chief Superintendent of the Royal Ordnance Factory, Woolwich, whilst his Assistant CME, A. C. Stamer, became acting CME of the NER in his absence. In 1916 Thompson joined Raven at Woolwich, but was shortly afterwards appointed to the Movements Branch of the Directorate of Transportation in France, in a post which carried the Army rank of lieutenant-colonel. He was twice mentioned in despatches and was awarded the OBE. Peppercorn also went to France. He was commissioned into the Royal Engineers and became technical assistant to the Chief Mechanical Engineer of the Directorate of Transportation. Vincent Raven was in 1917 knighted for his services at Woolwich and appointed Deputy Controller of Armament Production at the Admiralty.[4]

In 1919 Thompson returned to his post as Superintendent of the Great Northern Carriage & Wagon Works, but in 1920 he went back to the North Eastern as Carriage & Wagon Works Manager at York. It is not clear why he left Doncaster to take up a parallel appointment at York. There may have been a difference of opinion with Gresley, but on the other hand the York Carriage & Wagon Works were much bigger than those at Doncaster and the post was probably more highly paid. At York Thompson introduced an adaptation of the conveyor belt system of assembly which had been initiated for cars in America by Henry Ford. The York system worked well and the establishment was visited by railwaymen from all over Europe.

Peppercorn, when he came back from France, was appointed District Locomotive Superintendent at Retford; and in 1921, a year after Thompson's departure from there, he became assistant to the new Carriage & Wagon Superintendent at Doncaster.

At the end of 1922, then, on the eve of the birth of the London & North Eastern

Railway, the two principal characters of this
book were both on the carriage and wagon
side of their respective railways.

Notes
1 FF. A. S. Brown; *Nigel Gresley: Locomotive
   Engineer;* Ian Allan Ltd, 1961, pp12-15
   Peter Grafton; *Edward Thompson of the LNER;*
   Kestrel Books, 1971, pp11-17
2 J. F. Harrison, letter to the author
3 Grafton, op cit, p18
4 ibid, pp19-20

Below left: E. Thompson. / *Crown Copyright/National Railway Museum, York*

Below: A. H. Peppercorn. / *Crown Copyright/National Railway Museum, York*

3. LNER-The First Five Years

In his new appointment Gresley had a large number of railway works under his control. There were: the Doncaster Plant Works of the Great Northern Railway; the North Eastern Locomotive Works at Darlington and Gateshead; the North Eastern Carriage Works at York, and Wagon Works at Shildon; the Great Eastern Works at Stratford; the North British Works at Cowlairs, Glasgow; the Great Central Locomotive Works at Gorton, Manchester; the Great Central Carriage and Wagon Works at Dukinfield, Manchester; and the Great North of Scotland Works at Inverurie, north of Aberdeen.

The amalgamations were followed by a number of resignations and new appointments in the Chief Mechanical Engineer's department. Sir Vincent Raven of the North Eastern effectively retired, but was retained for a year as Technical Adviser to the LNER. A. C. Stamer, who had been acting CME of the North Eastern in Raven's absence, became Assistant CME of the LNER and remained at Darlington. A. J. Hill of the Great Eastern retired and C. W. L. Glaze, who had been Works Manager at Stratford, became District Mechanical Engineer, Stratford. J. G. Robinson of the Great Central retired and his assistant at Gorton, R. A. Thom, was appointed District Mechanical Engineer, Gorton. W. Chalmers of the North British remained at Cowlairs as Mechanical Engineer Southern Scottish Area, and T. E. Heywood of the Great North of Scotland remained at Inverurie as Mechanical Engineer and Running Superintendent Northern Scottish Area. In 1925, however, Chalmers retired and the opportunity was taken to combine the two Scottish Areas. R. A. Thom was moved to Cowlairs as Mechanical Engineer Scotland, whilst Heywood replaced Thom at Gorton. O. V. S. Bulleid was in 1923 appointed Principal Assistant to the CME, and in the same year A. H. Peppercorn became Carriage and Wagon Superintendent at Doncaster. In 1924 B. Spencer was appointed Technical Assistant to the CME. In 1927 Edward Thompson was moved to Stratford as Assistant Mechanical Engineer, where Glaze used him primarily on works organisation. He was succeeded at York by Arthur Peppercorn.

After the Grouping construction continued of a number of locomotives to the designs of the old companies. Stratford, for instance, was busy building the so-called 'Super-Clauds', the 10 with the 5ft diameter boiler, and the N7 0-6-2 tank engines. From Darlington came more of the P3 (J27) 0-6-0s, the S3 (B16) 4-6-0s, and the T3 (Q7) 0-8-0s. Construction at Cowlairs had stopped in 1921, when the passage of the Railway Act foreshadowed the end of the North British as an independent railway. As a result, however, there was a serious shortage of locomotives in Scotland. To help meet the deficiency, Gresley sent north the 15 superheated Great Northern 4-4-0s of Class D1, some K2 two-cylinder 2-6-0s, and a number of the N2 0-6-2 tanks. As a more powerful engine than the 'Scott' was needed for the intermediate passenger services, Gresley, to save time, ordered the construction of 24 of the Great Central 'Improved Directors', or D11 class 4-4-0s. They had proved very satisfactory in service and were the most modern of that wheel arrangement immediately available in design. Great Central engines also appeared on the old North Eastern, for some of the A5 4-6-2 tanks were built to meet a shortage of locomotives for the Darlington-Middlesbrough-Saltburn and other services. In 1924 Darlington began building the Great Northern type K3 three-cylinder 2-6-0s. Sixty were built in 1924-25, differing from the original 10 Great Northern engines in having a North Eastern side-window cab.

It is noteworthy that all the engines which Gresley designed, as well as those of the former Great Central which he rebuilt, had round-top fireboxes. He gave the following explanation for this in his Chairman's address to the Leeds Branch of the Institution of Locomotive Engineers on 11 May 1918:

'In the case of almost every railway which has adopted the Belpaire box, the firebox roofs of their old round-topped boilers were stayed by roof bars, which are well known to be objectionable on account of the difficulty in keeping the firebox free from dust. Naturally, when they introduced Belpaire boxes with direct roof stays, many of the troubles disappeared, and the improvement was put down to the adoption of the Belpaire-type boiler . . . I have come to the conclusion that, from a maintenance standpoint, the Belpaire boiler offers no advantage over the direct-stayed, round-topped boiler, whilst undoubtedly its first cost is greater.'

This was not an argument with which G. J. Churchward would have agreed, because it neglected his contention that the Belpaire firebox gave increased steam space and water surface. However, the round-top firebox remained an LNER standard until the end of that Company's existence.

Brief mention was made in Chapter 1 of the trouble experienced with the valve gear of the three-cylinder 2-6-0 No 1000. Because this matter of valve gear played such an important part in the design of Gresley's three-cylinder engines, and was the principal reason for criticism of them by his successor,

it is perhaps worthwhile giving a brief explanation of valve gears generally, and of Gresley's in particular, for the benefit of the non-technical reader.

The function of the valve is, of course, to admit steam to each end of a cylinder in turn, to force the piston in that cylinder to move alternately forwards and backwards. It also provides a path for the used steam to escape from the cylinder through the blast pipe and chimney to the atmosphere. The valve moves in a chamber known as the steam chest, which is supplied with steam from the boiler.

The slide valve was the type in almost universal use up till the end of the last century. This moved over a flat surface in

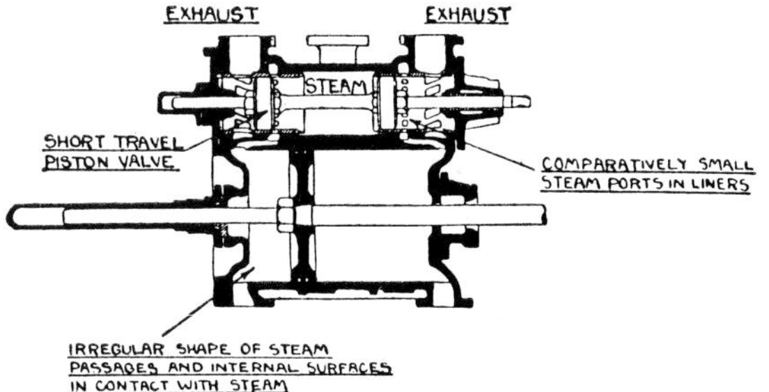

Above : Old Pattern Cylinder and Valve.
Below : Cylinder Valve and Piston of New Standard Locomotives, L.M.S.R.

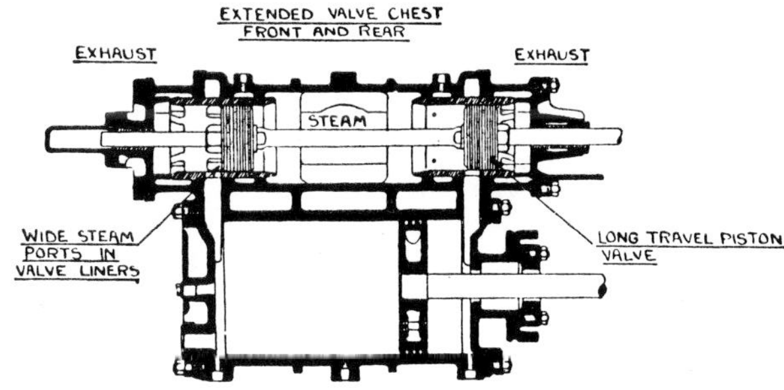

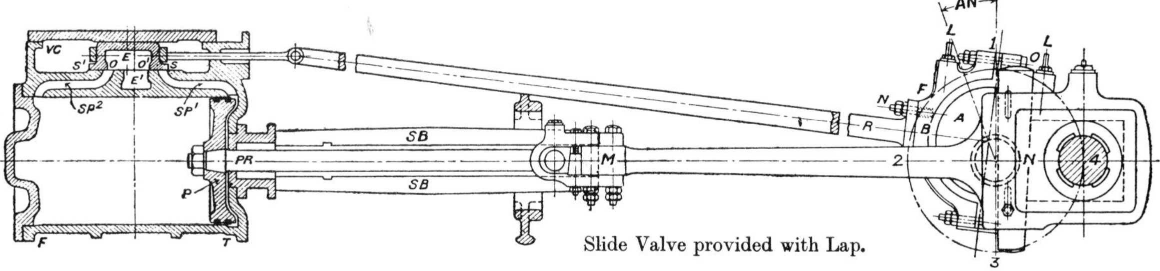

Slide Valve provided with Lap.

which there were three ports — the two outer communicating with the two respective ends of the cylinder and the middle one connecting with the blast pipe. The outer ports had the dual function of admitting steam from the steam chest to the cylinder and then exhausting it through the middle port. The movement of the valve was so arranged that the paths for the live and exhaust steam were opened and closed at the required times. The earliest valve gears admitted steam to the cylinder for the whole of its working stroke. This was very wasteful and the invention of an adjustable valve gear enabled the steam to be cut off at varying proportions of the stroke so that the expansive qualities of the steam could be used. In order to be able to cut off the steam early and also to secure a later exhaust, the outside edges of the valve were extended to overlap the ports, which of course gave the valve a longer distance to travel. The additional length of valve face across the ports was called 'lap'. In order that the steam should enter the cylinder in time to exert its full effect on the piston as soon as it began its stroke, the valve was made to open the port to steam a little in advance of the commencement of the stroke, and the amount of this opening was called 'lead'.

When steam was admitted for most of the piston's stroke, the travel of the valve was long enough to open the ports to their full extent for both the admission and the exhaust of the steam. But reducing the period that steam was admitted (to make maximum use of expansion) entailed shortening the travel of the valve and the ports were no longer fully opened. The result of this was that the steam was throttled at admission, and there was back pressure from the exhaust. It was possible, however, to give the valve a much longer travel, combined with longer laps, so that wide ports were still obtained when the engine was 'linked up'. But slide valves are heavy things and engineers were reluctant to give them a very long travel on account of the increased wear. The ideal way of driving an engine is with the regulator fully open (because this gives unrestricted steam flow from boiler to cylinders) and with the 'cut-off' (ie the period during which steam is admitted

before the valve cuts it off) as short as possible. With short travel valves it is not practicable to have short cut-offs because the port openings become too small, and it was customary to drive such engines with a moderate cut-off and a partially opened regulator. This was bad because the steam flow from boiler to steam chest was throttled, with the result that the pressure in the steam chest was well below that of the boiler.

The invention of the piston valve made possible a revolution in engine working. Its potentialities were realised comparatively early, but there were difficulties in making it steam tight, which were not solved until after the beginning of the present century. The force required to move a piston valve is only about one sixth of that needed for a slide valve. G. J. Churchward, the eminent Locomotive Superintendent of the Great Western Railway, was the first in this country to appreciate that this removed the objection to long travel valves, and to the valve gear which was consequently evolved at Swindon much of the success of Great Western engines was due.

Piston valves have two piston heads connected by a rod, moving inside circular liners fitted into the cylindrical valve chest. Steam is normally supplied from between the piston heads and exhausted at the two ends of the valve chest — the reverse of the slide valve arrangement.

There are a number of different types of gear which have been devised to operate the valves. By far the most widely used in latter days has been the Walschaerts. In this the movement of the cylinder crosshead is combined with that of an eccentric on the driving axle, or a return crank on the engine crank pin, to produce the valve travel. The eccentric, or return crank, is connected by an eccentric rod to the bottom of an expansion link. In this link there slides a block which is the terminus of a radius rod, and the position of this block determines the movement of the radius rod from maximum forward through neutral to maximum reverse. The position of the block is controlled by the driver's operation of the reversing gear, which is attached to the radius rod by a lifting link.

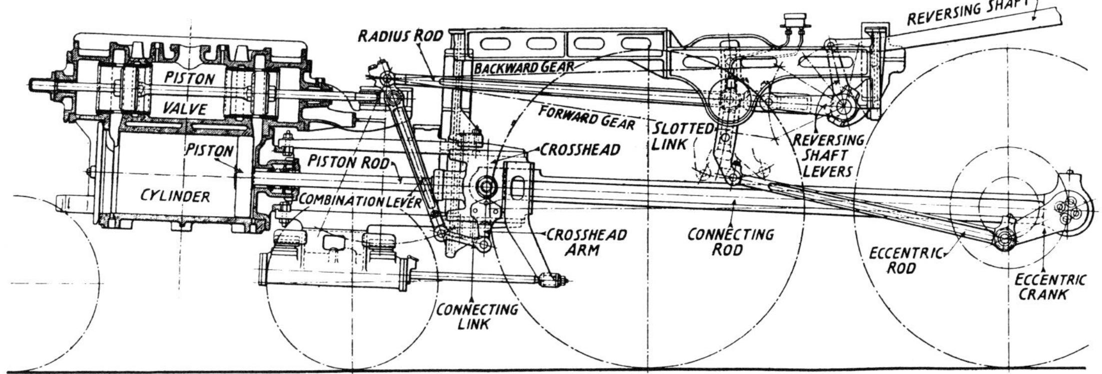

Walschaerts' Valve Motion applied to Outside Cylinders of a Modern Express Locomotive.

The other end of the radius rod is connected to a combination lever, of which the top end is attached to the valve spindle and the bottom end, through a union link and the crosshead arm, to the crosshead. Most of the movement comes from the crosshead, but from the radius rod comes the length of the cut-off and the direction of travel.

For a three-cylinder engine one could have three sets of Walschaerts valve gear, but to avoid the extra mechanism between the frames Gresley preferred that the valve of the middle cylinder should be operated by a motion derived from the valve gear of the two outside cylinders. The gear that he eventually adopted was derived from one invented by H. Holcroft, who, as he told the author, collaborated with Gresley in its ultimate design. In this gear the valve spindles are extended beyond the front of the cylinders. One outside valve spindle is connected to one end of a short lever pivoted at its centre. The other end of this lever is connected to the inside cylinder valve spindle. The other outside cylinder valve spindle is attached to one end of a long lever, which is pivoted at a point distant two-thirds of its length from this valve spindle. The other end of this lever carries the fulcrum for the short lever. Movement of the inside cylinder valve is thus derived from the movement of the two outside cylinders.

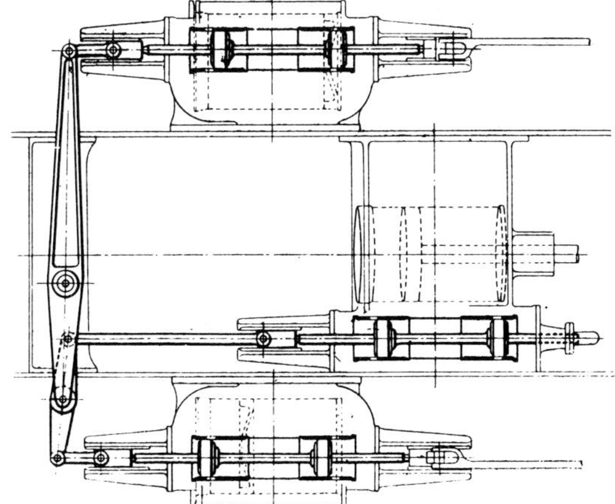

The Gresley Valve Gear in Plan.

Holcroft told the author that he wanted this conjugated gear arrangement placed behind the cylinders. This is not possible unless the inside cylinder drives on the leading coupled axle, because to clear that axle it has to be steeply inclined. Gresley did not like driving on the leading coupled axle, except on a four-coupled locomotive, because this made it impossible to provide the lateral play on the leading coupled axle which he thought to be essential. This ruled out a divided drive, which he did not like anyway. The gear, therefore, had to be put in front of the cylinders, with unfortunate results. The trouble was that any slackness in the pins and joints of the gear was emphasised in its effect on the movement of the inside-cylinder valve spindle, and this was increased at speed by whip in the action of the levers. Hence the over-travel in which the middle-cylinder valve spindle crosshead struck and damaged the steam chest cover. If the gear could have been placed behind the cylinders this would not have happened. As it was, and as related in Chapter 1, Gresley limited the maximum valve travel on his first Pacifics, to eliminate the damage, by reducing the cut-off in full gear to 65%, instead of the normal 75%. The disadvantage of this was that it reduced the tractive effort at starting and there were sometimes difficulties, particularly when starting a heavy train from a sharply curved platform, such as at York or Newcastle.

Without his conjugated gear Gresley would probably have found it difficult to get his undivided drive. One advantage of the gear was that, the crosshead connection of an independent valve motion being unnecessary for the inside cylinder, the crosshead could be placed close to the leading axle so that the inclined cylinder could be kept well clear of the base of the smokebox. There would not indeed have been room to fit a Walschaerts valve gear to a cylinder inclined at 1 in 8.

Trials between the Gresley and Raven Pacifics clearly established the superiority of the former and it was accordingly selected as the standard heavy express passenger engine for the LNER. Gresley's engines did not show so well in trials which took place in 1925 between them and the 'Castle' class 4-6-0s of the Great Western Railway. The 'Castles' were C. B. Collett's larger-boiler version of G. J. Churchward's famous four-cylinder 'Stars', and their most noteworthy features were Churchward's excellent boiler and his long travel and long lap valves. The superiority shown by the Great Western engines led eventually to the fitting of long lap and long travel valves on the LNER Pacifics, with a consequent reduction of the average coal consumption on a 500 ton train between Doncaster and Kings Cross from 50lb per train mile to 38lb. The valve travel at 65% cut-off was increased from $4\frac{9}{16}$in to $5\frac{3}{4}$in and the lap from $1\frac{1}{4}$in to $1\frac{5}{8}$in for the outside cylinders and $1\frac{11}{16}$in for the inside.[1] The new gear was designed by Spencer. (The longer lap on the inside cylinder valve was intended to equalise the work between the three cylinders, because, due to the imperfections of the conjugated gear, the centre cylinder did more work than the others at high speeds.[2])

The first engines which Gresley designed for the London & North Eastern Railway were the two three-cylinder Class P1 2-8-2s of 1925 which were intended to work 1,600 ton mineral trains between Peterborough and London. They were developed from his Pacifics and had the same boiler. A booster was fitted on the trailing carrying wheels to assist on starting or when checked on a gradient. However, the booster was subsequently removed because the engines could handle longer trains than the Operating department could manage. Another engine of 1925 was the solitary 2-8-8-2 Garratt locomotive with six cylinders for banking on the Worsborough branch with its gradient of 1 in 40. The cylinders and most of the running gear were interchangeable with the O2 three-cylinder 2-8-0s.

In 1924 Gresley had a design prepared at Doncaster for a 2-6-0 goods engine with 5ft 2in wheels and a K3 type boiler to replace the various 0-6-0s of pre-Grouping design. The scheme was abandoned;[3] it may be that there were insufficient turntables of suitable length for an engine which was intended for very wide use. Instead Darlington was instructed by Gresley to plan a two-cylinder 0-6-0 goods engine based on the North Eastern P3 class (J27), but with wheels of 5ft 2in instead of 4ft 7½in. However at this time more powerful locomotives were badly needed for the Fifeshire coal trains, so that the first batch of these engines were turned out in 1926 with 4ft 8in wheels (a LNER standard size) and were classified J38. The generally similar 5ft 2in engines appeared later in the same year and were classified J39. There were eventually 289 J39s, the most numerous of Gresley classes. Apart from their Doncaster chimneys, the engines were typically North Eastern in appearance — cab, smokebox saddle, and the single curves on the running plate were all Darlington features. The J39s were used on a wide variety of duties: slow and fast goods, excursion, and semi-fast passenger trains. They were very successful, but with their unguided coupled wheels they suffered badly from axlebox wear and needed much maintenance.

The Great Central 'Directors' had been doing good work in Scotland, but as more intermediate express passenger engines were needed both there and in the North Eastern area, Gresley decided to meet the requirement with a more modern type and directed Darlington to plan a three-cylinder 4-4-0 with the J39 boiler. The new engines were classified D49 and were to be powerful enough to supplement the North British Atlantics on routes such as Edinburgh to Aberdeen and Edinburgh to Carlisle over which the Pacifics at that time were not allowed to run. The choice of the J39 boiler was probably influenced by the chronic need on the LNER for economy. Like the J38s and J39s, the D49s were predominantly North Eastern in line and detail. The three cylinders drove on the leading coupled axle and this made it possible to place the conjugated valve gear behind them and so avoid the trouble which arose from having them in front. The first engine was completed in September 1927, and as the whole batch of 36 were named after English or Scottish counties, they were popularly known as the 'Shires'.

In 1925 Gresley had started experimenting with Lentz poppet valves. In that year a Great Eastern 0-6-0 was fitted with them, and the results were sufficiently promising for seven of the Great Eastern B12 4-6-0s to be similarly converted. There was sufficient reduction in coal consumption for 10 more of this class to be built in 1928 with Lentz valves for the London-Southend services. The poppet valves of all these engines were actuated by oscillating cams. In 1928 six of the D49s were fitted with Lentz poppet valves, also with oscillating cams driven by Walschaerts valve gear and the conjugated arrangement to operate the centre cylinder camshaft. However, the centre cylinder valve events proved difficult to maintain and the engines were given piston valves when the cylinders needed renewing.

In 1929 two of the 'Shires', No 336 *Buckinghamshire* and No 352 *Leicestershire*, were fitted with poppet valves driven by a rotary cam gear, designed by Lentz in collaboration with the LNER. A comparison between piston valve engines and those with OC and RC Lentz poppet valves showed the last as being a little lighter on coal used per drawbar horsepower. Forty more D49s with RC Lentz poppet valves were therefore built between 1932 and 1935.[4] These engines were all named after hunts.

The D49s, both piston-and poppet-valve engines, proved competent in service, but their rough riding made them unpopular with the enginemen. The early promise of the poppet valves was not confirmed in practice, and some trials carried out in 1935-6 showed a piston-valve engine to be much more economical over a wide range of power at ordinary running speeds than two competing poppet-valve engines.[5]

Gresley had been impressed with the work of André Chapelon of the Research and Development Section of the Paris-Orleans Railway. In 1926 Chapelon designed his Kychap exhaust — so-called because it was derived from an exhaust gas and steam device invented in 1919 by a Finnish engineer named Kylala. Chapelon's object was to produce an adequate draught over the whole smokebox and to mix the gases so well with the exhaust steam that the mixture might be expelled with the minimum of effort. From the top of the exhaust standpipe, leading from the cylinders, the exhaust steam passed through a conical blast pipe nozzle fitted with four radial wedge-shaped inserts. These inserts divided the steam into four jets which, drawing some of the hot gases with them, passed into the four lobes of the Kylala spreader which was mounted a short distance above. This division of the steam into four jets improved still further the entrainment of the hot gases above the exit of these lobes, where more of the hot gases circulated; the mixture was then carried upwards through a petticoat to a final mixing with the remainder of the gases and out through the chimney.[6]

Trials of the Kylchap exhaust on the PO gave remarkable results and in 1928 Gresley

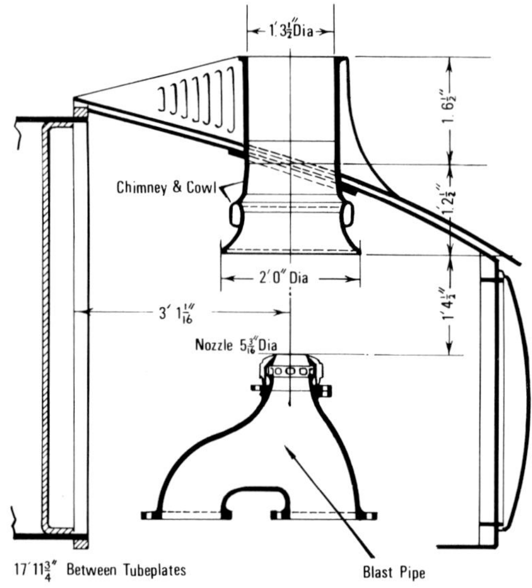

The interior of the smokebox of the Class A4 with the single chimney and with the Kylchap double chimney. The blastpipe orifice was originally $5\frac{3}{16}$in in diameter and the two Kylchap orifices were each 5in in diameter.

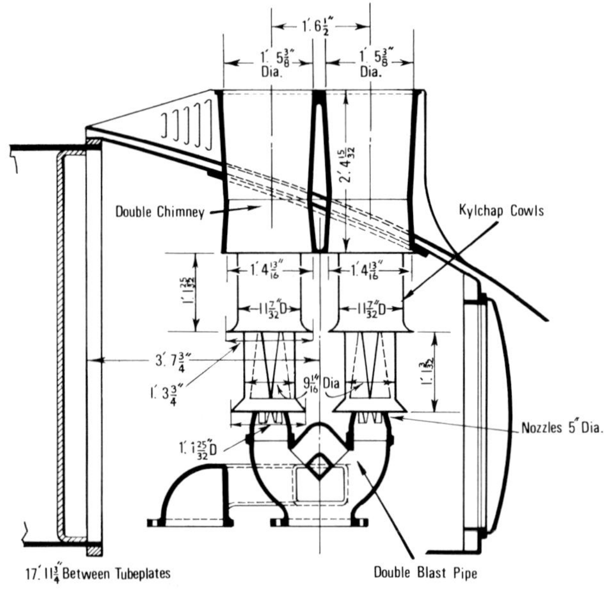

obtained drawings from the PO so that he could try out the device himself. (This was before Chapelon's outstanding rebuilding of Pacific No 3566 in 1929, which was to astonish the locomotive world and was to have a profound influence on all subsequent LNER design.) By October 1928 No 251 *Derbyshire* had been fitted in Darlington Works with a Kylchap exhaust. First reports were good and in January 1929 Darlington was ordered to fit a similar exhaust to an OC Lentz poppet valve engine, No 322 *Huntingdonshire*, and this was completed in April 1929. In the meantime Chapelon had ridden on the footplate of No 251 and found that it was not steaming as well as it should. He found that the lobes of the Kylala spreader had been connected by stays (which somebody at Darlington had apparently thought was a good idea) and that this was affecting the flow of the gases adversely. In addition the petticoat was out of centre with the chimney. Oddly enough Darlington had also fitted these stays on No 322, so that they had to be removed from both engines. No further D49s were given the Kylchap exhaust and it was removed from both engines in 1930. Obviously the trials had been of value as both Gresley and his successors used the Kylchap exhaust extensively on the P2s and the later Pacifics.

Notes

1   B. Spencer; 'The Development of LNER Locomotive Design 1923-1941', *The Journal of the Institution of Locomotive Engineers*, vol XXXVII (May-June 1947)
2   The Railway Correspondence & Travel Society, *Locomotives of the LNER*, Part 2A, p13
3   F. A. S. Brown; *Nigel Gresley: Locomotive Engineer*; Ian Allan Ltd, 1961, p93
4   Spencer, op cit
5   RCTS, *Locomotives of the LNER*, Part 4, p93
6   Colonel H. C. B. Rogers; *Chapelon: Genius of French Steam*; Ian Allan Ltd, 1972, pp22-23

Above right: J39 class 0-6-0 No 2727. / *Ian Allan Library*

Right: J39 class 0-6-0 as BR No 64770 on the 11am Parkeston to Goodmayes continental goods train. / *E. R. Wethersett*

L N E R
2727

64770

Top right: 'Shire' or D49 class three-cylinder 4-4-0 No 234 *Yorkshire.* / *LPC*

Right: Class D49 No 62731 *Selkirkshire* leaving How Mill on a Newcastle to Carlisle stopping train in August 1956. / *R. Leslie*

Below: Gresley P1 2-8-2 No 2394 trundles a lengthy freight up through Potters Bar in 1929. / *E. R. Wethersett*

4. In Which Thompson Makes His Mark

Perhaps the principal LNER locomotive milestone of 1928 was the appearance of the A3 class Pacifics (the earlier Gresley type being at this time classified as A1 and the Raven variety as A2). The decision had been taken in the previous year to construct Pacific boilers with an increased number of superheater flues and a pressure raised from 180-220psi. Trials with the new boiler showed its superiority as compared with the original pattern, and construction of the first batch of Pacifics fitted with it and classified A3 began in August 1928. Between 1922 and 1925 52 Great Northern type A1 Pacifics had been built, and by 1935 there were 27 of the A3s. A1s were subsequently converted to A3 when they required new boilers.

At this time the Great Eastern section was in need of more powerful passenger locomotives than the B12 4-6-0s. Owing to the weight restrictions on the lines of the old Great Eastern these engines had comparatively small boilers, and they had consequently to be worked so hard that coal consumption was heavy and maintenance costs were high. The principal limiting factor was the weakness of the underline bridges over which a maximum axle load of only 15 tons was allowed for a two-cylinder engine. As the Doncaster design staff were heavily engaged, Gresley gave the problem to the North British Locomotive Company. They produced a three-cylinder 4-6-0, but with divided drive to bring the weight on the middle coupled axle down to 18 ton 7cwt,

which the Civil Engineer was prepared to accept for an engine with three cylinders. Because the drive was divided, it was possible to put the conjugated gear behind the cylinders, as on the D49s. The first of these 4-6-0s, the B17 or 'Sandringham' class, was completed in 1928. The North British Locomotive Company built ten of them and construction was then handed over to Darlington, where 52 were built from 1930 to 1936. In 1937 a final 11 were built by Robert Stephenson & Company in their Darlington Works. In many respects the 'Sandringham' was a six-coupled version of the 'Shire'. The last 25 of these useful engines went to the Great Central section to replace the 'Directors' on the London expresses and had standard tenders instead of the small Great Eastern pattern.

In 1929 there was completed at Darlington Works Gresley's remarkable high pressure four-cylinder compound 4-6-4 locomotive No 10000, the sole representative of Class W1. It had a water-tube boiler with a pressure of 450psi. In spite of early promise the engine proved difficult to maintain and not nearly so economical in coal consumption as the Pacifics. It was weak during acceleration when working compound after a stop because it took some time to build up the superheat, so that the low-pressure cylinders were doing little work owing to condensation and the high-pressure cylinders alone could not provide sufficient power. The principal maintenance difficulty lay in keeping the boiler walls airtight because of the variation in the temperature of the plates, with the consequence that air was drawn through the defective joints, instead of through the grate, and steaming suffered.[1] Both Gresley and Bulleid had discussions with Chapelon on what could be done to improve the engine. Chapelon pointed out that the degree of superheat was insufficient to avoid condensation in the low-pressure cylinders and that it should be increased. He added that even better results could be obtained by re-superheating between the high-pressure and low-pressure cylinders, and that the fitting of a Kylchap exhaust would help. In May 1935, therefore, No 10000 returned to

Darlington Works where it was fitted with a double Kylchap exhaust and resuperheat. Performance and efficiency were improved, but the lack of air tightness remained a problem and in 1937 the engine was rebuilt as a three-cylinder simple with a conventional boiler.[2]

Also in 1929 two of the Great Central Class O4 2-8-0s were rebuilt with Great Northern Class O2 round-top firebox boilers in place of their Belpaire type. The rebuild was found to be successful and 10 years later a considerable number were similarly modified.

In the latter part of 1930 the first of 82 Class V1 2-6-2 tank engines were turned out from Doncaster, with three cylinders driving the middle pair of coupled wheels and the conjugated valve gear in front of the cylinders. They were intended primarily to take over the heavy suburban services in the Edinburgh area and between Glasgow and Helensburgh from the North British 4-4-2 tank engines, which were in need of replacement. In 1939 10 more were built, but these had a boiler pressure of 200psi instead of the 180psi of the earlier engines and were classified V3. This was the only new tank engine design during Gresley's time as Chief Mechanical Engineer of the LNER.

In 1930 Edward Thompson succeeded Glaze as Mechanical Engineer Stratford. Peter Grafton relates[3] that he and his wife occupied a flat off Baker Street, and that sometimes in the evening he would walk to Paddington station to watch Great Western engines at work. As a result of these visits he asked A. E. English of his technical staff what made the exhaust from Great Western engines sound like shots from a gun. English replied that it was due to their sharp valve events with long valve travel, combined with a high boiler pressure and the resonance of a small smokebox. Thompson then asked him what savings there would be if one of the Great Eastern 4-6-0s was converted to long travel valves. English (doubtless with knowledge of the results achieved on the Pacifics) replied that there might be a 25% reduction in coal consumption. It seems curious that Thompson should have been apparently unaware of the comparative tests carried out in 1927 between Pacifics with short and long travel valves and the subsequent fitting of all Gresley Pacifics with the latter.

Trouble was being experienced in 1932 with the B12 4-6-0s which had Lentz poppet valves, because the cylinders of this 1911 design were not standing up well to the hammering of these valves and were starting to crack. Thompson got authority to rebuild them as piston valved engines and seized the opportunity to use a long valve travel. He recommended, too, that as the B12 Belpaire boilers of many engines needed renewal the opportunity should be taken to replace them with the larger 'Sandringham'-type boiler with a round-top firebox.

The design of the valve gear was entrusted to English. Experiments were carried out on B12 No 8559, which had piston valves. These engines had Stephenson's valve gear for their two inside cylinders, and the valves being above the cylinders got their motion from a rocking lever pivoted at its centre. The valve travel on No 8559 was increased from the original $4\frac{3}{16}$in to $6\frac{1}{16}$in by moving the point of pivot so that the top arm of the lever was longer than the bottom arm. In the light of the very encouraging results, English embarked on a thorough re-design of the gear. A full size mock-up was erected at Stratford, and Thompson himself would turn the handle which operated it whilst English worked out the dimensions.

When all was ready one of the 1927 poppet valve engines was rebuilt with English's new valve gear and a B17 boiler. The engine was so successful that Gresley approved a large-scale rebuilding. By December 1933 all the poppet-valve B12s had been rebuilt, and subsequently nearly three-quarters of the piston valve engines were given the new valve gear and B17 boilers. One of them, No 8535, was the first engine to achieve a speed of 90mph on the lines of the old Great Eastern Railway.[4]

Thompson, of course, deserves full credit for his part in the rebuilding of the Great Eastern B12 4-6-0s. It has been suggested, however, that he was responsible for the design of the rebuild and to have even carried out the work without Gresley's full knowledge. This seems most unlikely. The trouble with poppet valves must (or should) have been brought to Gresley's notice, and it is inconceivable that the engines should have been rebuilt with short-travel valves in 1932. English, as we have seen, designed the valve gear, and the only other major part of the rebuilding was the fitting of an existing standard boiler. An interesting aspect of the rebuilding was that it was found possible to use the bigger boiler without increasing the weight on the axles above that allowed by the Civil Engineer for a two-cylinder engine. The weight of the original B12s was 63 tons and the rebuilt engines weighed 69 tons 10cwt. The three-cylinder B17s were nearly eight tons more.

The success of the B12s led to an even more complete reconstruction of the 'Claud Hamiltons'. The B12s had been piston-valve engines from the start, but the 'Clauds' had always had slide valves. Rebuilding of these engines with larger boilers having round-top fireboxes and some with long travel piston valves began late in 1932 under Thompson's supervision. Where the existing cylinders and slide valves were in good condition, however, they were retained. They were such good engines that, except where cylinders were in need of renewal, the extra cost of conversion was presumably not worth while.[5]

In 1933 A. C. Stamer retired and Edward Thompson went to Darlington to replace him as Mechanical Engineer, North Eastern Area. If the Grouping had not taken place, this was the year in which Thompson would probably have succeeded Stamer as CME of the North Eastern Railway. Before Thompson left Stratford, Arthur Peppercorn arrived there as Assistant Mechanical Engineer. Life must have become pleasanter for this amiable and kindly man when his autocratic and difficult chief departed for Darlington, for Thompson was difficult. In his running of Stratford he had no idea of man management. His relations with the men under him were appalling, he would walk round the Works without ever condescending to notice them, let alone talk to them. He had a quiet speaking voice about which he was sensitive and was liable to lose his temper with any unfortunate subordinate who dared to ask him to repeat a statement. He was neurotic, and there was an extraordinary instance of this after he had had an attack of jaundice. He ordered the temperature of his office to be kept within certain limits and had thermometers installed to make sure that this was done. One day he returned from lunch to find the thermometers registering a temperature which was above the limit he had laid down. In a temper he picked up a cast iron paper weight from his desk, hurled it through one of the double glazed windows; then, storming into his clerk's office, he ordered him to get the damage repaired.[6] One suspects some lack of mental balance. Certainly there was nothing in Thompson's character to appeal to that great extrovert and leader of men, Nigel Gresley.

Nor was Gresley over-blessed with tact. He did not spare Thompson in public, if he thought his ideas were poor — and they often were — and criticism of him in front of others was something that Thompson could never forgive. Gresley discussed his locomotive policy with Thom (now Mechanical Engineer at Doncaster) and Bulleid. Thompson felt out of it, and brooded accordingly.[6]

Notes

1 B. Spencer; 'The Development of the LNER Locomotive Design 1923-1941', *The Journal of the Institution of Locomotive Engineers*, vol XXXVII (May-June 1947)
   F. A. S. Brown; *Nigel Gresley: Locomotive Engineer*; Ian Allan Ltd, 1961, pp104-106

2 Colonel H. C. B. Rogers; *Chapelon: Genius of French Steam*; Ian Allan Ltd, 1972, pp41-42
   K. Hoole; *North Road Locomotive Works*; Roundhouse Books, 1967, pp46-47

3 Peter Grafton; *Edward Thompson of the LNER*; Kestrel Books, 1971, p31

4 O. S. Nock; *The Locomotives of Sir Nigel Gresley*; The Railway Publishing Company, 1945, pp108-113
   Brown, op cit, pp122-123
   Grafton, op cit, pp31-32
   Cecil J. Allen; *The London & North Eastern Railway*; Ian Allan Ltd, 1966, pp129-130
   Cecil J. Allen; *The Great Eastern Railway*; Ian Allan Ltd, 3rd edn, 1955, pp143-145

5 Brown, op cit, pp118-120
   Nock, op cit, p113
   Allen, GER, pp132-133

6 J. F. Harrison, letter to the author

Left: LNER Class A3 Pacific *Isinglass* as BR No 60063 on a semi-fast train for Peterborough in April 1955. / *Brian Morrison*

Below: Class A3 Pacific No 60100 *Spearmint* with Kylchap exhaust and double chimney and German pattern smoke deflectors on a Kings Cross to York at Peterborough North in August 1961./ *P. H. Wells*

Right: A3 Pacific No 60052 *Prince Palatine*, standing in for a failed diesel locomotive, leaving Carlisle on the 1.45pm train to Edinburgh over the Waverley Route./ *S. C. Crook*

Centre right: B17 or 'Sandringham' class three-cylinder 4-6-0 No 2848 *Arsenal*. / *Ian Allan Library*

Bottom right: B17 class 4-6-0 No 2840 *Somerleyton Hall.* / *LPC*

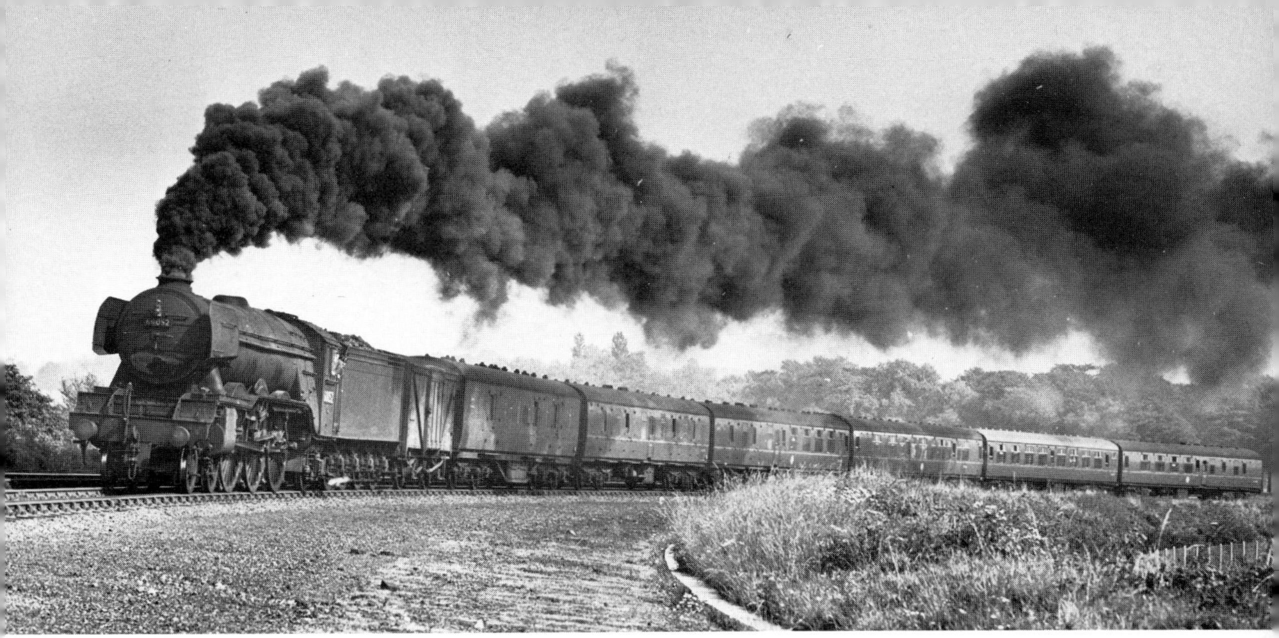

ARSENAL
2848
L N E R

2840
L N E R

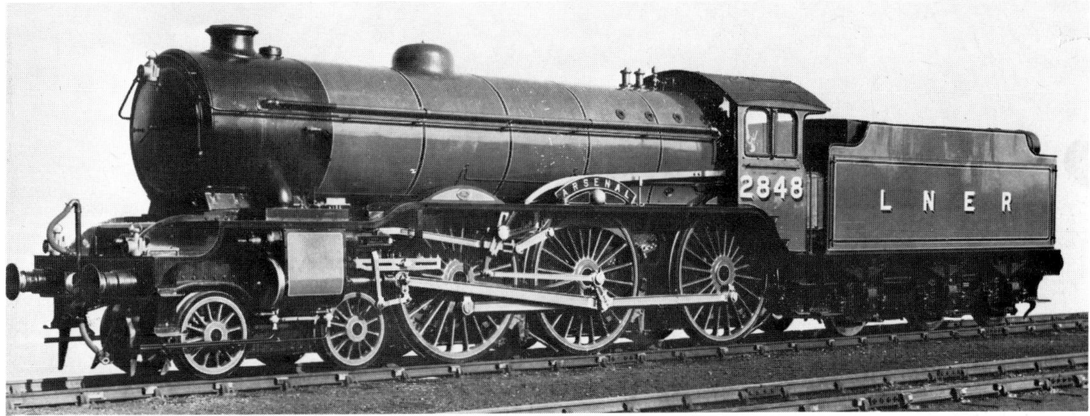

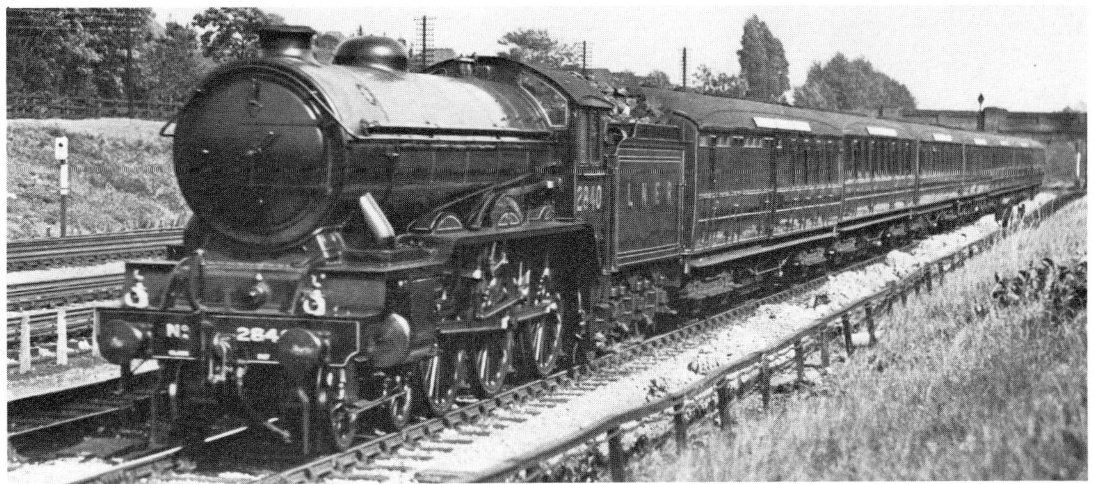

Above left: V1 class 2-6-2 tank engine No 67626 on the 4.17pm Queen Street to Helensburgh train in July 1955. / *I. S. Pearsall*

Left: GER 1500 class 4-6-0 in early LNER days. No 1539 on a down Yarmouth express. / *Ian Allan Library*

Above: GER 1500 class 4-6-0 as LNER B12 class No 8515 / *Crown Copyright*

Right: GER 4-6-0 No 8516 rebuilt as Class B12/3, with improved valve gear and B17 boiler, seen near Chadwell Heath in 1933. / *E. R. Wethersett*

Above: Class B12/3 4-6-0 No 61570 at Stratford in May 1957.
/ *R. E. Vincent*

Right: Class B12/3 4-6-0 No 61577 pulling out of Lincoln Central with a special for Driffield on 14 May 1959.
/ *E. R. Wethersett*

Below right: V3 2-6-2T No 451 gets away from Cambridge past Trumpington with a slow train for Liverpool Street on 11 August 1945.
/ *E. R. Wethersett*

5. Bogies and Blastpipes

Between 1930 and 1934 no new locomotive design was produced for the LNER, but in May of the latter year the first of the P2 three-cylinder 2-8-2 express locomotives appeared from Doncaster. It is necessary to consider this engine in some detail because of Thompson's later rebuilding of the P2 class. It was noteworthy in two respects: it was the first time in Great Britain that this wheel arrangement had been used for an express locomotive and it was the first design in which full use was made of the lessons derived from Chapelon's rebuilding of the Paris-Orleans Pacifics.

The P2 class was intended to meet the traffic needs of the winding curves and heavy gradients of the main line between Edinburgh and Aberdeen. The A3 Pacifics were limited to 480 tons northbound and 440 tons southbound, whilst an engine was wanted which could handle 550 tons in either direction. No 2001 *Cock o' the North* had internal, wide-diameter, streamlined steam passages, following Chapelon's practice, together with a Kylchap double exhaust and an ACFI feed water heater. Lentz poppet valve gear was fitted, operated by oscillating cams. Originally these cams were continuous: that is to say, they allowed an infinitely variable cut-off, like piston valves. After some 10,000 miles of running, service trouble developed in the follower rollers of the valve mechanism. Stepped rotary cams were accordingly substituted with the valve events limited to six ranges of cut-off in forward

gear. However, with the engine's high tractive effort, there was a large difference in power between each cut-off position. This was uneconomic, and No 2001 burned more coal than the second engine, No 2002, which had piston valves.

No 2001 had aerodynamic screening in order to lift the soft exhaust which resulted from the low back pressure, rather similar to that which had been adopted for No 10000, so that there was some similarity in the appearance of the two engines.

In December 1934 *Cock o' the North* went over to France for trials at the Vitry test plant. The trials proved disappointing because, like many other engines, No 2001 could not be driven hard on the test plant without the axleboxes overheating. Gresley, worried about this, visited Chapelon in his Design Office, showed him the plans of the engine, and asked what he should do. Examination did not reveal any particular fault and Chapelon proposed a trial on the line with a test load. The load, in accordance with normal PO practice, consisted of a dynamometer car and three 'dead' four-cylinder compound counter-pressure locomotives (in which water is admitted to the cylinders and pumped against pressure in the boiler). The test took place between Les Aubrais and Tours. In contrast with the test bank troubles, the engine ran satisfactorily without any heating of the axleboxes and showed itself capable of a drawbar horsepower of 2,000 at 70mph. This was, however, far inferior to the 3,600 equivalent drawbar horsepower developed by one of Chapelon's four-cylinder compound 4-8-0 locomotives at 61mph. Chapelon noticed on the trials that *Cock o' the North* was very hard on the track owing to the first coupled axle of the rigid wheel base encountering any change in direction too roughly. This was particularly noticeable at the junction of Montlouis, which was taken rather harshly even by Chapelon's own Pacifics. The trouble could have been overcome, he considered, by using an Italian bissel bogie, by which a displacement of the leading truck was followed by a lateral movement of the leading coupled axle. This arrangement he fitted to his own 141.P class 2-8-2 locomotives, which rode as well as the Pacifics whilst having superior adhesion. This solution was in fact proposed to Gresley by an engineer, Richard Pennoyer, who had ridden on the footplate of Italian 2-6-2s and 2-8-2s which had the Zara bissel bogie. Gresley replied that he had considered this, but felt that it was not desirable to introduce a new and rather complicated suspension system on a small class of locomotives which already included numerous innovations.[1]

Bulleid, in the discussion following Spencer's previously mentioned paper, said of *Cock o' the North's* visit to France that the engine was 'extremely efficient on the testing plant, and compared favourably with the French engines in her coal consumption per rail-hp, and, better still, per dbhp. When tested on the open road between Orleans and Tours she developed a very high horsepower, of the order of 2,800, and again showed herself to be an efficient engine from the point of view of coal consumption per dbhp.' Bulleid, however, was speaking 13 years after the event and his memory appears to have been at fault. In fact, the comparative test figures on the open road between one of Chapelon's rebuilt Pacifics and *Cock o' the North* were as follows:[2]

	PO Pacific		*Cock o' the North*
Speed	68mph	56mph	68mph
dbhp	1,910	2,700	1,910
Water per hp/hr	7.5kg	8.20kg	10.45kg
Coal per hp/hr	1.05kg	1.22kg	1.48kg[2]

Gresley himself had no illusions about the results of the tests. He told the Institution of Locomotive Engineers that the first *Cock o' the North* would be the last and that any subsequent P2 class engines would embody the lessons learned in France.

The second of the class, No 2002 *Earl Marischal*, was completed in October 1934 before the despatch of No 2001 to France. She differed from the earlier engine in having piston valves with Walschaerts valve gear and Gresley's conjugated gear for the middle cylinder. Side deflector plates had to be fitted to lift the soft exhaust. In 1936 four more were built with piston valves, and these did indeed incorporate improvements suggested by the comparative trials with the French locomotives. They included larger steam passages (which had already been embodied in the A4 class Pacifics) and the double Kylchap exhaust (which the A4s did not have originally). The aerodynamic screening was dropped in favour of the form of streamlining devised for the A4s, and this solved the problem caused by the soft exhaust failing to lift the smoke clear of the cab windows. On the A1 and A3 Pacifics there was usually a drop of 10psi between the boiler and the steam chests, but on these later P2s there was no drop at all. Nos 2001 and 2002 were subsequently altered to conform with Nos 2003 to 2006. These otherwise excellent engines were spoiled by their rigid wheelbase, because the curving route of the Edinburgh-Aberdeen main line, particularly near Montrose, led not only to continual trouble with hot axleboxes on the coupled wheels but to side pressure spreading the track.

Gresley's magnum opus, the A4 class Pacifics, arose from the requirement for a locomotive to haul a high-speed train between Kings Cross and Newcastle. The engine was a further development of the original Great Northern Railway Pacifics, embodying not only improvements in the light of British experience but also the internal streamlining of the steam circuit derived from a study of Chapelon's practice. In addition the engine was streamlined externally because it was calculated that this would save about 10% in power output. (It is, of course, conceivable that the publicity value of streamlining may have played a part in this decision!) Strangely enough the Kylchap double exhaust was not adopted and instead of it Gresley chose Churchward's jumper blastpipe top. The first engine, No 2509 *Silver Link* was completed at Doncaster in September 1935. An interesting innovation was the bogie, and in view of the subsequent troubles experienced with bogies under Thompson and Peppercorn, it is worth discussing the development of bogies under Gresley. The original bogies fitted to Gresley's Pacifics were very similar to those designed by Ivatt and used on his famous Atlantics.

In general a bogie is required to turn about a pivot and also to have some lateral movement. Its essential function is to guide the locomotive round curves, and it must have adequate springs or other arrangement to restore it to its normal position — otherwise it will be merely a flexible truck without giving any assistance to the leading coupled wheels. There have been many different types of bogie designed to meet these requirements, of which some have been extremely good and others extraordinarily bad.

H. A. Ivatt brought his bogie from the Great Southern & Western Railway of Ireland and used it on his first Great Northern 4-4-0 engines of 1896 and subsequently on the Atlantics. It was based on one designed by Alexander McDonnell for his 0-4-4 tank engines of 1870 when he was Locomotive Superintendent of the GS&WR. After proving satisfactory on these engines he fitted it to his 4-4-0 'Kerry' engines of 1877. J. A. F. Aspinall adopted the same design when he succeeded McDonnell, as did Ivatt, when in his turn he succeeded Aspinall in 1886.

Side movement of this bogie was controlled by swing links. On the A1 Pacifics these links were 7in long between pivots, allowing a side movement of $3\frac{1}{2}$in. In fact this sideplay was not enough for the Pacifics, because their wheelbase was longer than that of the Atlantics, and in 1927 it was increased to 4in. The D49 class 4-4-0s had an entirely different type of bogie, which had been designed at Darlington and which had helical spring side control instead of swing links. In 1931 Gresley tried this bogie on an A1 Pacific, and it proved so successful that in August 1932 he decided that all the Pacifics should be provided with it, though with some slight modifications. When the A4s appeared they too had the D49-type bogie, with side control springs having an initial loading of 2 ton and a maximum loading of 4.55 ton at 4in throwover. This loading, however, proved insufficient, as was shown by excessive wear on the flanges of the leading coupled wheels. The initial loading was therefore increased to 4 ton and the maximum to 7 ton.[3]

This type of bogie had one disadvantage as compared with the swing link pattern in that it did not prevent excessive rolling. At Gresley's invitation, R. C. Bond rode on the footplate of an A4 from Kings Cross to Newcastle and back. Bond told Gresley that he thought the A4s very fine engines, but said that they did not ride as well as Stanier's Pacifics because they occasionally rolled badly at high speed, so that the driver had to brake. (Bond formed the impression that nobody had dared to tell Gresley this before.) Gresley asked Bond what the reason was, and he replied that he thought it was the bogie. Gresley thereupon sent to Stanier, through Bond, a request for the drawings of the LMS bogie.[4] Tests made in 1938 confirmed the correctness of Bond's diagnosis and the LMS system of side checks on the bogies was adopted. These were horizontal check plates fitted to the undersides of the main frames and the tops of the bogie frames on both sides of the engine. There was normally a gap of $\frac{1}{16}$in between the check plates, but any roll to one side was checked by the plates coming into contact with one another.[5]

In 1938 four of a new batch of A4 Pacifics were given the double Kylchap exhaust, and it was one of these, No 4468 *Mallard*, which achieved the world record for steam traction of 126mph. However, theoretical studies at Doncaster threw doubt on the value of the Kylchap system and no more A4s were fitted with it at this stage. Nevertheless, the Kylchap exhaust played such an important part in the later LNER locomotive policy that the whole history of its use on the A4 Pacifics had perhaps better be recounted here, even though it takes us into the final period of steam on British Railways.

Blastpipes have been the subject of much controversy, and of them K. R. M. Cameron has said: 'There has probably been more steam blown off in the metaphorical sense then ever passed through the blastpipes themselves.' His own view is that any well-designed blastpipe system is good provided that the smokebox is kept airtight, the tubes and brick arch are kept clean, and the fuel is of good quality. 'The Kylchap', he says, 'proved itself superior when fuel quality fell off from first-class standard, and the double blastpipe fitted to the A4s later in their life did give an improvement in their steaming.' At Kings Cross, Cameron says, they tried many things to improve the steaming. He got into official hot water for clamping down the jumper tops, even though this did improve the steaming on several A4 engines. 'The A4', he adds, 'was a magnificent machine provided it was kept in first-class order: there was never a mediocre A4; it was either brilliant or it was b——— awful! They were like racehorses in that they demanded attention if you were to get the best results.'[6]

At the time that he was Assistant District Motive Power Superintendent at Kings Cross, P. N. Townend had no doubt about the value of the double Kylchap exhaust. When he went to Kings Cross in 1956 the A4s were, and had been for some time, he says, at a low ebb in performance. 'The depot had either bolted down the jumper top blastpipes or fitted their own fixed tops of various heights and sizes, but none of these was satisfactory and could not be in comparison with the three A4s at Kings Cross which had always had the Kylchap arrangement.' Townend asked for the double Kylchap exhaust to be fitted to all the A4s, but encountered considerable opposition. The Chief Mechanical and Electrical Engineer tried, instead, an alteration of the chimney cowl, etc, to the proportions used on the Western Region and asked for a report on the engines so treated. Townend submitted a report with a conclusion that the Western Region arrangement compared unfavourably with the Kylchap exhaust and that it was this that they wanted. However, the response to this report was another set of Western Region proportions. The first lot had been based, says Townend, on a Dean 0-6-0 and the amended ones were only a slight variation of these. Townend felt that it was essential to have the Kylchap exhaust if he was to improve the A4s because 'the Western Region proportions only made magnificent noises, which was a sure sign of what was wrong!'

Local authority also opposed the Kylchap double exhaust. Townend was told that the double blastpipe could not be fitted without a new middle cylinder casting. He promptly instructed a fitter at the shed to measure everything in the smokebox of two locomotives — one with the double Klychap arrangement and the other without — and to let him know what was needed to change the latter over to a double Kylchap exhaust. The fitter's answer was, 'Undo four nuts and make a bigger hole in the top.' Townend was also told; 'You don't want all that gubbins in the smokebox, as you cannot clean the tubes.' He comments ironically that no one seemed to know how the tubes of the Kylchap engines had been cleaned for nearly 20 years. However, to counter this objection he obtained a compressed air gun that would blow them out from the firebox end.

At about this time an enquiry received from the British Railways Board as to whether it was true that the A4s with the Kylchap did not steam properly, and if so would Kings Cross like them removed. Townend replied that the engines steamed excellently and that they would like all the A4s converted to this system. No action resulted, however, from this request.

The Interchange Trials had shown the double-chimney A4 to be the most economical of all the locomotives tested, and so it was decided to put up a case from the Depot direct to the General Manager for the conversion of all A4s, not already so fitted, to the double Kylchap exhaust on account of the coal that this would save. It was possible to do this because the CM&EE did not control the depots. As the Depot did not have the use of the dynamometer car, they could only measure the coal used with any accuracy by comparing double-and single-chimney locomotives in similar mileage conditions on the same round working to Doncaster. Initially the required results could not be obtained because the driver of the Kylchap-fitted locomotive was too enthusiastic, making up time all the way and arriving early. In order to get a true comparison of the respective fuel consumptions, the Inspector was asked to curb the enthusiasm of the driver of the Kylchap engine and instruct him to maintain strict sectional times, shutting off and coasting whenever possible. The Kylchap engine then showed an economy of from 6 to 7lb per mile as compared with the single chimney one. The results were reported to the General Manager, who agreed readily to instruct the CM&EE to fit a double Kylchap exhaust to all the A4s. The cost was just over £200 per locomotive, which the saving in coal would soon recover. Similar comparative tests were carried out on A3 Pacifics. There was a slightly lower coal saving of 5 to 6lb per mile, but it was sufficient for the General Manager to direct that these engines, too, should be fitted with the double Kylchap, at a cost which came to only £153 per locomotive.[7]

'Having achieved this', Townend writes, 'and the V2s having all the indications of requiring to be freed at the front end, tests were made with a V2; but unfortunately, as most firemen knew, the V2 was a very economical locomotive and burnt less coal than the double blastpipe A3, though barely keeping time with the train, so a case could not be made based on savings in coal.'[8]

The three-cylinder V2 class 2-6-2 locomotives had been designed to meet a need for an engine more suited than the K3 2-6-0 for express goods and passenger services. The first of them, No 4771 *Green Arrow*, left Doncaster Works in June 1936. The following year construction of V2s started at Darlington, and eventually 159 out of a total of 184 engines were built there.

Of the V2s at Kings Cross, Townend says that No 60845 had been redraughted at Swindon, and it was considered by the authorities that this redraughting should put the V2s right; 'but', he adds 'it missed the main advantage we were getting from the Kylchap locomotives.' Eventually the Depot obtained authority to equip two locomotives with double blastpipes, but the type authorised was the British Railways standard pattern, which did not include the Kylala spreader and other Kylchap fittings. These two double blastpipe V2s were not noticeably better than a good single-chimney V2. Further pressure was then exerted to get at any rate some of these engines fitted with the Kylchap arrangement. It was urged that V2s had to stand pilot at Peterborough station to cover Deltics and Pacifics because longer engines could not be turned there, and it was essential that a pilot should be at least capable of not losing any more time. In response to this argument, approval was given for six V2s to have the Kylchap double exhaust. Of these, one or two were always at Peterborough for the main-line pilot jobs, and three or four were usually at Kings Cross for the 'lodge turns' (ie the express freights to York), the working of which they improved considerably.

The first of the Kylchap V2s came up to Kings Cross with a Doncaster Inspector, who was most enthusiastic about it. He said that he had to stop the driver from going over 100mph! Townend concludes:

'Without a doubt the fitting of the Kylchap exhausts made the task very much easier on our main line, particularly in the changeover to diesels. The Pacifics as a whole did better day-by-day work than they had ever done, and were running Kings Cross-Newcastle and back in 12 hours on diesel diagrams, which had never been done before, and day after day as necessary. In fact, in one four-weekly period at the time a Pacific did more miles than any of the diesels on the main line in that particular period (over 11,000). Perhaps the feeling from the enginemen is that of the Sectional Council member at Peterborough, who said to me that it was not diesels they wanted but double blastpipes. Mileages of the Pacifics increased considerably between overhauls, but other things helped to achieve this. 70-80,000 was about the maximum at one time, but out of the 19 A4 locomotives allocated after double chimneys were fitted, six were still at work at mileages of 100,000 at one time and one at 130,000.'[9]

There remains to be mentioned the last locomotive construction to be carried out during Gresley's period as CME. In October 1936 one of the North Eastern R class 4-4-0s (LNER D20) was rebuilt at Darlington under Gresley's direction, with long travel piston valves of increased diameter. The boiler mountings were unaltered, but the engine suffered somewhat in appearance through the raising of the running plate for the whole width of the coupled wheel splashers. Thompson was directly responsible for the carrying out of the work. He incurred Gresley's wrath, however, by releasing information about the engine to the Press without first consulting him. Gresley, in typical fashion, gave Thompson a verbal dressing down as soon as he saw him, irrespective of the presence of some of the latter's subordinates. This was something that the proud and neurotic Thompson could never forgive. The engine was successful and three more were rebuilt, though without the external alteration, and they did not appear until after Gresley's death.[10] As these rebuilds were very good engines, one would have expected that the same treatment would have been afforded to many more of the class. It is conceivable, however, that Thompson had conceived an intense dislike of the engine which had been the cause of his discomfiture.

The rebuilding of the R class 4-4-0 was followed by that of one of the North Eastern S3 class (LNER B16) three-cylinder 4-6-0s. The North Eastern boiler, chimney, and dome were retained; but the rebuilt engine had new cylinders and, instead of three sets of Stephenson's valve gear, there was Walschaerts gear for the outside cylinders and the Gresley derived motion for the middle cylinder. The drive of all three cylinders was on the leading coupled axle, so that the conjugated gear could be placed behind the cylinders. Six others were subsequently rebuilt in the same way.

At this time a need had arisen for more powerful engines for the West Highland than the Great Northern K2 class two-cylinder 2-6-0s, which had been drafted there to work the heaviest trains on the line. However, they were limited to a maximum load of 220 tons. Owing to the increasing weight of the trains this limit was frequently exceeded, and double-heading (generally by two of the North British 'Glen' class 4-4-0s) became necessary. To cope unassisted with these trains, Gresley designed a three-cylinder 2-6-0 with 5ft 2in coupled wheels and a 5ft 6in diameter boiler. The object was to provide an engine with a tractive effort 50 per cent greater than that of the K2s, without exceeding the bridge loading limits imposed by the Civil Engineer. Larger wheels were unnecessary because there was a speed limit on the West Highland line of 40mph. The first of this new K4 class, No 3441 *Loch Long*, was completed at Darlington in March 1937. In June 1937 its boiler pressure was increased from 180-200psi to facilitate faster uphill working. The engine was a brilliant success and could handle 300 ton trains. Five more were built in 1938 and 1939.

In March 1938 Thompson was appointed to succeed R. A. Thom as Mechanical Engineer Doncaster and took up his new post on 1 July 1938. Mrs Thompson, however, died before the move took place. Peppercorn had become Locomotive Running Superintendent of the LNER Southern Area in 1937, and he was promoted to succeed Thompson as Mechanical Engineer Darlington.

Gresley's last design was the V4 2-6-2 class, of which only two were built, going into service in 1941. It had been LNER policy to use engines, which had been supplanted on the main line, to operate secondary main and branch-line services. The V4 was Gresley's attempt to provide a modern three-cylinder mixed traffic engine, with a high route availability, to meet these needs. It incorporated all the successful features of his previous express and mixed traffic engines, together with a maximum axle load of 17 tons, which was light enough for it to run over 5,000 of the LNER's 6,414 route miles. On test the engines proved very successful on both express and freight train workings.

On 5 April 1941 Sir Nigel Gresley died suddenly of heart failure shortly before reaching his 65th birthday. Many people have assumed that Gresley would have retired at the age of 65. In fact, it is probable that he would have liked to have gone on till he was 70, and the LNER Directors held him in such high estimation that they would have undoubtedly have welcomed such a request. This would have taken him on to 1946, when it was planned, no doubt at Gresley's suggestion, that J. F. Harrison who would then have been 42, should succeed him. But in 1941 Harrison was too junior in the LNER hierarchy. Thompson was the most senior and had the necessary contacts as well as previous war experience, but he was already aged 60. It was perhaps with some reluctance that the Directors decided to appoint him CME. At any rate they divested him of some of the authority that had been vested in Gresley, and responsibility for Electrical Engineering was, to Thompson's disgust, removed from the CME and made into a separate department with H. W. Richards as its chief.

Gresley was certainly a difficult man to follow. He had risen rapidly to a pre-eminence amongst locomotive engineers. At a time when the Great Western was resting on the laurels of Churchward and the LMS was still handicapped by Midland small-engine policy, Gresley had provided the LNER with a stud of big locomotives which were actually in advance of traffic requirements and which were unmatched in performance until Sir William Stanier's massive re-equipment of the LMS. The achievement was the greater in that the LNER was always in a state of financial stringency, and the Board kept a very close rein on the money it allowed its CME to spend. Hence Gresley's use and rebuilding of pre-Grouping locomotives, rather than the new construction that he would have preferred. He was no advocate of standardisation, believing that it led to stagnation, and his engines were largely 'tailor-made' for the job; witness, for example, the K4 class designed specifically for the West Highland line, the P2s for the Edinburgh-Aberdeen service, and the J38 0-6-0s for the East Fife coalfields. If he spent money on experimental work, it was minute in comparison, for instance, with the vast sums spent by British Railways in recent years on the Advanced Passenger Train. Nor were his locomotives unduly expensive; indeed, the cost of construction of his Pacifics was markedly lower than that of the major express locomotives of other lines.

The most controversial part of his work was his addiction to three cylinders whenever possible, with his conjugated gear to operate the valve of the middle cylinder. How this worked and some of the difficulties experienced with it were mentioned in Chapter 3. T. C. B. Miller says[11] that the three cylinders of the K4 2-6-0s gave them the high tractive effort that was needed on the West Highland line, so that double-heading by 'Glens' (whenever the trains were too heavy for a single K2) could be dispensed with. On the other hand B. C. Symes thought that Gresley pressed the three-cylinder design too far, and the little V4 class 2-6-2 *Bantam Cock* (and its sister) was a very expensive engine for the work it was intended to perform 'though no doubt it pleased the Civil Engineer!'[12] K. R. M. Cameron thought that the adoption of an independent Walschaerts gear for the middle cylinder was an unmitigated improvement. Maintenance of the conjugated gear, especially on the A4s, was a constant source of worry, and it always seemed to him extraordinary that the pins on the conjugated motion of the A4 class were smaller than those of the earlier A3, and did not therefore wear so well. The only part of the independent valve gear of the Peppercorn A1 engines which did give a certain amount of trouble was the middle eccentric sheave, but with careful maintenance this could be kept under control.[13] Nevertheless Gresley had good historical support for adopting a derived gear. The compound Pacifics built for the PLM Railway of France after World War I had a derived gear for the inside cylinders because it was noted that four independent sets, as used on the earlier compound Pacifics, were more expensive to maintain than the gear of the simple expansion Pacifics which used a derived motion for the inside cylinders.[14]

Symes, in the drawing office at Doncaster, had to make a diagram showing how an assumed wear in the conjugated valve gear pins and bushes could mount up until it was about 11 times greater when it reached the middle valve. This was recognised in Gresley's time by the increase of the middle valve lap by $\frac{1}{16}$in more than the outside ones, so reducing the port opening to steam. Before the war Symes was fortunate in being chosen to go indicating on one of the A3 Pacifics. When speed rose to about 75mph and over, the middle cylinder was developing nearly half the horsepower instead of one third, due to the longer port opening which resulted from the cumulative clearance and whip in the two-to-one levers. He considers that this was probably one of the reasons why the middle big ends were so 'dicey'.[12]

But it would show a lack of proportion to emphasise the weaknesses in Gresley's engines, because when he died it could perhaps be claimed that he had left the LNER with the finest fleet of large locomotives in the country. He will be remembered chiefly for his magnificent A4 Pacifics.

Below: *Lord President* on an Edinburgh and Aberdeen express. / *Ian Allan Library*

Notes

1 H. C. B. Rogers; *Chapelon: Genius of French Steam*; Ian Allan Ltd, 1972, pp42-43
   G. W. Carpenter, letter to the author
2 Rogers, op cit, p43
   B. Spencer; 'The Development of the LNER Locomotive Design 1923-1942', *The Journal of the Institution of Locomotive Engineers*, vol XXXVII (May-June 1947)
3 ibid
4 R. C. Bond, information to the author
5 The Railway Correspondence & Travel Society, *Locomotives of the LNER* Part 2A, p102
6 K. R. M. Cameron, letter to the author
7 P. N. Townend, letter to the author
8 ibid
9 ibid
10 Peter Grafton; *Edward Thompson of the LNER*; Kestrel Books, 1971, pp39-40.
11 T. C. B. Miller, conversation with the author
12 B. C. Symes, letter to the author
13 Cameron, op cit
14 L. M. Vilain; *L'Evolution du Materiel Moteur et Roulant de la Cie Paris-Lyon-Mediterranee*; Vincent et Cie 2nd edn, p137

Top: A4 class No 2509 *Silver Link*, built 1935. The first of the class. / *LPC*

Above: P2 class 2-8-2 No 2003 *Lord President*, built 1936 with Kylchap exhaust and double chimney.

Right: A4 class Pacific No 4491 *Commonwealth of Australia* entering Kings Cross on the 'West Riding Limited'. / *H. Gordon Tidey*

Top: A4 class Pacific No 2512 *Silver Fox*, with the emblem of the fox below its name. / *Ian Allan Library*

Above: A4 class Pacific No 60019 *Bittern* with double Kylchap exhaust and skirting plates removed at Perth on 5 July 1965. / *Ian G. Holt*

Right: A4 class Pacific No 60029 *Woodcock* with the down 'Yorkshire Pullman' at Marshmoor 11 July 1953. / *E. R. Wethersett*

Far right, top: V2 class 2-6-2 No 4771 *Green Arrow*, as restored, leaves York for Harrogate with a test train on 15 March 1978. / *L. A. Nixon*

Far right, bottom: No 4771 *Green Arrow* on the 3.55pm down Scottish Goods in 1936. / *LPC*

Right: Class D20 (NER Class R) 4-4-0 No 2020 rebuilt with long-travel piston valves in 1936. / *Ian Allan Library*

Below: Class B16 (NER Class S3) rebuilt with new cylinders and Gresley's gear as B16/2: No 61435 at Hull Dairycoates on 15 July 1964. / *D. Hardy*

Far right, top: K4 class 2-6-0 No 3441 *Loch Long*, built in 1937 for the West Highland line. / *Ian Allan Library*

Far right, bottom: K4 class 2-6-0 No 61995 *Cameron of Lochiel* on the 4.50pm Fort William to Mallaig train at Banavie. / *E. D. Bruton*

LOCH LONG
3441
L N E R

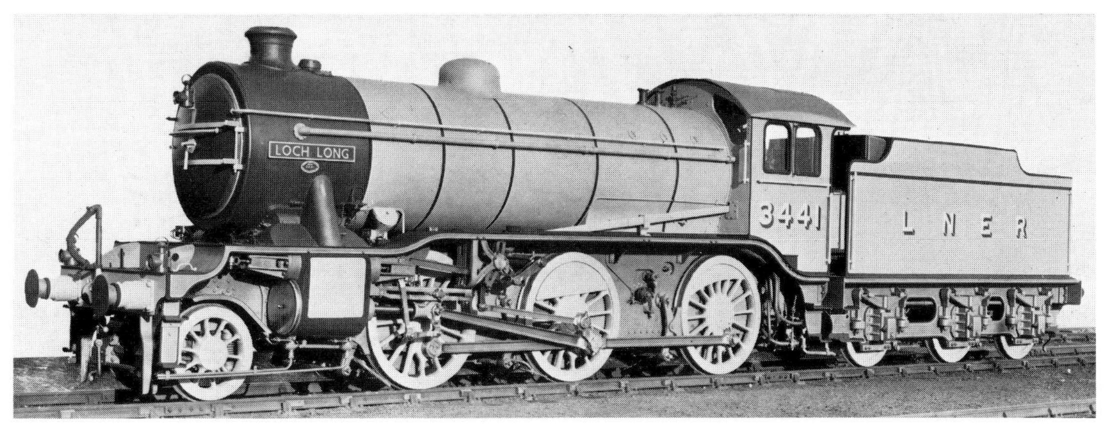

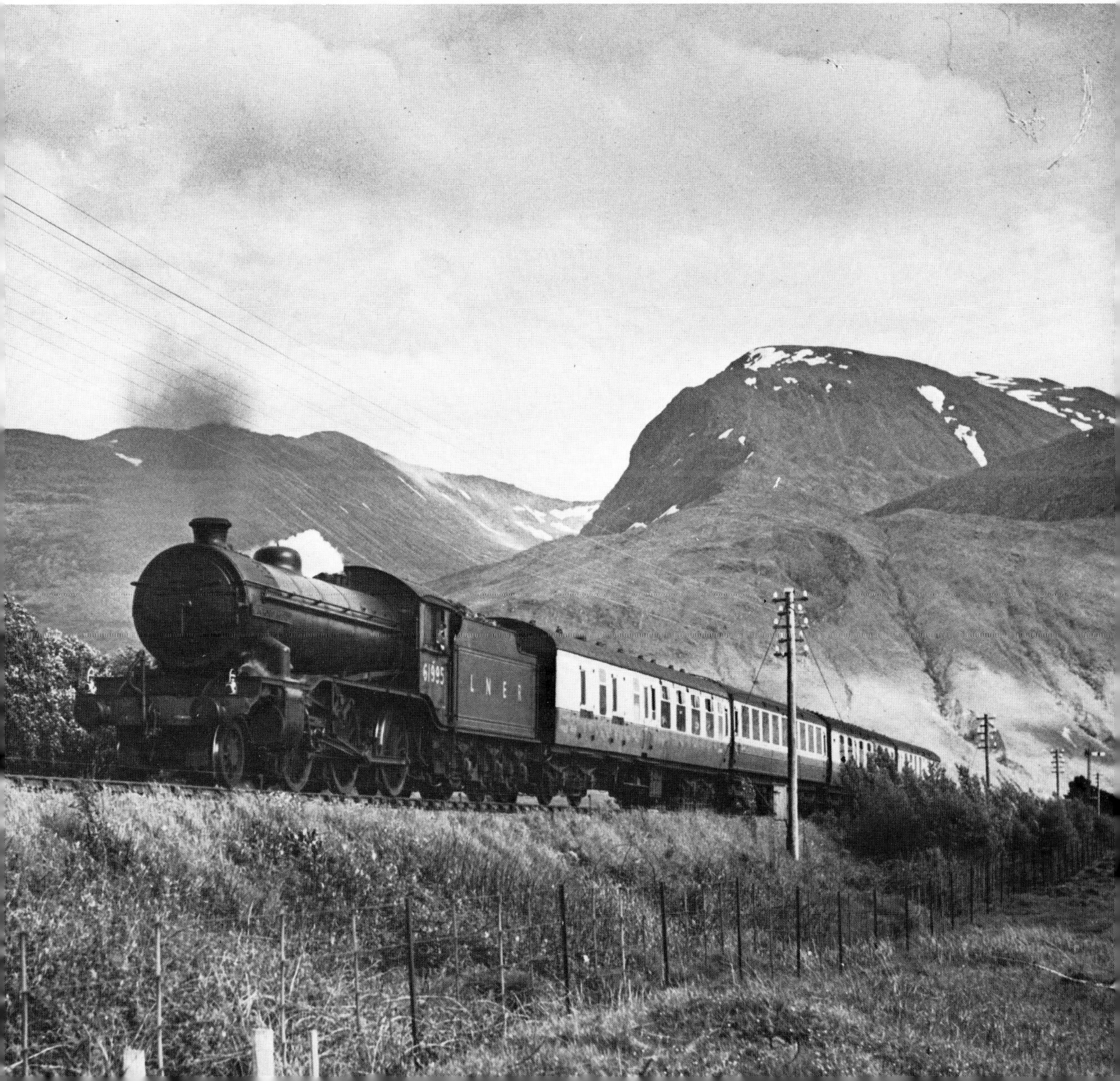
61995
L N E R

Above right: A rare shot of V4 class 2-6-2 No 3401 *Bantam Cock*, built 1941, on trial with the 8.20am ex-Liverpool Street, near Trumptington on 21 August of that year. / *E. R. Wethersett*

Right: Bantam Cock on the 3.46pm Glasgow to Fort William train in Glen Douglas 1944. / *Ian Allan Library*

Below: A4 4-6-2 No 4496 with old numbering but with valences removed and renamed *Dwight D. Eisenhower.* / *E. R. Wethersett*

6. Thompson Takes Control

It is important to remember that it was during the darkest days of World War II, on 28 April 1941, that Edward Thompson was appointed Chief Mechanical Engineer of the London & North Eastern Railway. Standing alone against the Axis Powers, the country was struggling for survival — a struggle which most of the world thought was destined to end in defeat. The railways formed an essential part of that struggle and the keystone of the railway arch was the motive power that kept the traffic moving.

The LNER was the fortunate possessor of more modern big locomotives than any other company, but it did not have a sufficient number of modern engines for its secondary passenger and freight services. This, as we have seen, was due to the Company's continual shortage of money, which had led to the retention of many of the pre-Grouping locomotives. A large number of these were wearing, or were worn, out. The need to replace them had been appreciated before the outbreak of the war; and it will be remembered that Gresley introduced the V4 2-6-2 for this specific purpose. Under the conditions prevailing before the war, the V4, if a rather expensive solution to the problem, would probably have been a very successful engine. But under wartime conditions something simpler was needed because it was no longer possible to keep up the same standards of maintenance. Many of the company's skilled artisans had been enlisted in the fighting Services, locomotive works were having to undertake an increasing amount of armament manufacture, and multiple manning of locomotives was necessary, with sometimes two or more crews taking over in succession in the course of a single long-distance run. In 1941, then, and to see it through the war, the LNER needed a class of general purpose locomotives, similar to the LMS Class 5 and the GW 'Hall', which would be easy to operate and simple to maintain — and lots of them.

During Gresley's time the CME's office had been at Kings Cross. Thompson, who had been Mechanical Engineer Doncaster, decided to stay there (doubtless with the Board's approval) and he arranged his office accommodation accordingly. Shortly after his appointment he held a meeting at Doncaster which was attended by his senior staff. He concluded the discussion with the remark: 'I have a lot to do, gentlemen, and little time in which to do it.'[1] It must have seemed to his astonished audience that Thompson was more concerned with stocking the LNER with a complete range of his own designs during the five years' tenure of office which he could expect, than with the immediate wartime needs. His subsequent activities confirmed that impression.

Thompson had indeed outlined a scheme for a series of standard designs for LNER, in replacement of Gresley's policy of designing the engine for the job. There were, of course, sound reasons for a policy which had been pursued with success on both the LMSR and the GWR, but the middle of war was an odd time to make the change. Apart from the need of a general purpose engine, however, other requirements could probably have been met by building more of Gresley's very successful O2 2-8-0s and V2 2-6-2s. As it happened, Thompson refrained as far as possible from including any Gresley class amongst his standard engines. B. C. Symes writes[2] that when he was preparing his scheme for a complete stud of standard locomotives, Thompson 'browsed through the engine diagrams book which showed all the engines, including those of pre-Grouping design, and picked out those which by dimensions and tractive effort appeared suitable for conversion.' Symes adds that it was difficult to see any reason for some of his rebuilds of Gresley engines 'except to do away with everything Gresley'. He continues that as far as his standard designs were concerned, Thompson could hardly go wrong with the O1. 'It was the original GC 2-8-0 adopted in 1914 as the ROD engine, and 90 of them went overseas in the 1939-45 affair. By fitting them with modern cylinders (B1) and valve gear, and a B1 boiler, they had a still further lease of life.' In fact the O1 was virtually a new engine, for Harrison says that only the main frames and some of the wheel centres were retained. 'It was a first-class engine', he adds.

Of other rebuilds, Symes writes: 'The D49 rebuilt with two inside cylinders is a mystery — only one was done. The B17 rebuilt to B2 was in effect a B1 with larger coupled wheels and to my mind quite unnecessary. So far as the classes that Thompson selected for his rebuilding programme, I think there were too many. I do not think the A2 was required, in view of the V2 class; the J11 (rebuild of the GC 0-6-0) was not needed, in view of the K1 (two-cylinder rebuild of the K4); and we did not need *three* types of shunting tank, or the L1 passenger tank, as its work was quite adequately covered by the V1 and V3 types.' Symes draws attention to Thompson's strange choice of GC designs: a pre-1914 heavy goods engine, a light 0-6-0 of 1901, and a 0-8-0 of 1903 'converted to a heavy shunter which nobody wanted'. He adds that one would have expected him as a North Eastern man to have chosen from former NE types.

When Symes was in the drawing office at Doncaster, Thompson was frequently in it, discussing various points of design, 'and', he says, 'woe betide the unfortunate who did not hear what he said or ventured to offer an opinion'. Symes adds that 'Thompson had some little photo albums made by our photographers with a picture of one of his proposed standard engines on each alternate page and the engine diagram (line drawing with principal dimensions) on the facing page. One of these was given to each of the Directors and I saw a letter from one of them thanking him for "the beautiful little booklet" and expressing his pleasure at seeing the expert designs (or words to that effect). The same gentleman also expressed surprise that association with such masterpieces had not improved the character of his assistant [ie Peppercorn]! E.T. should have burned this, but there it was for anybody looking through the file to see.'[3]

Thompson's office staff suffered some discomfort from his autocratic methods. He had corridor panels reduced in height and panes of glass substituted for the upper portions so that he could walk along the corridor and see what was happening in the general offices. He supervised personally the siting of the office furniture and had the window sills rounded so that it was impossible to put anything on them. He was always the first to arrive in the morning and the last to leave in the evening, and he would periodically carry out an inspection of the offices after everyone else had gone home.[4] R. C. Bond remembers him at conferences when he liked to set out in front of him gold pencils, watches and other symbols of well-being. He adds that it was said of him that once he started calling a person by his Christian name it was the prelude to the sack![5]

After Thompson's appointment, Peppercorn was moved from Darlington to take up the new post of Assistant Mechanical Engineer and he was also made Mechanical Engineer, Doncaster. The other Mechanical Engineers were: Darlington R. A. Smeddle; Gorton, J. F. Harrison; Stratford, F. W. Carr; and Cowlairs, T. E. Heywood assisted by K. S. Ribertson. B. Spencer, Gresley's Assistant (Technical), was posted elsewhere and replaced by D. R. Edge, and D. D. Gray replaced T. E. Street as Head Locomotive Draughtsman. Future locomotive design was apparently to be inoculated against any danger of posthumous Gresley influence!

Because J. F. Harrison had so much to do with both Thompson and Peppercorn, and eventually succeeded the latter, it would be appropriate to give here a brief mention of his own remarkable career. Educated at Wellington College (where he was a school-fellow of the author), he went in 1921 to the Great Northern Railway, at Doncaster, as a premium apprentice. In 1923 he became a pupil of the then H. N. Gresley and during the following two years was a foreman at motive power depots. From 1926 to 1929 he was in charge of the old Great Central sheds at Wigan and St Helens. In 1930 he was moved to Gorton Locomotive Works as Assistant to the Works Manager, an appointment he held during the next seven years. In 1937 he was transferred to Doncaster as Assistant Works Manager, his chief being the ex-Great Central R. A. Thom. He was there only a year before he was back at Gorton on promotion to Locomotive Works Manager. Soon after he became CME, Thompson created the post of Mechanical Engineer (Great Central Section) Gorton, and to this Harrison was appointed. Looking ahead, Harrison remained at Gorton for most of Thompson's time as CME, but in 1945 he was transferred to Cowlairs as Mechanical Engineer (Scotland). In 1947 Peppercorn brought him back to Doncaster as Assistant CME LNER. In January, after Peppercorn's retirement, Harrison succeeded him; but the LNER had gone and his post was Mechanical & Electrical Engineer, Doncaster, British Railways, Eastern & North Eastern Regions. In July 1951, in accordance with the integration policy of British Railways, he was transferred to Derby as M&EE London Midland Region. In January 1955 the title of 'Chief' was restored to these appointments. In October 1958 Harrison became Chief Mechanical Engineer British Railways (Central Staff), thus reaching the highest appointment open to a locomotive engineer. In January 1965 the title was changed to that of Chief Engineer (Traction & Rolling Stock) British Railways and the responsibilities increased to include those previously exercised by the Chief Electrical Engineer. On 14 September 1966 Harrison retired.

Of Thompson, Harrison writes:[6]

'E.T. was in many ways an extraordinary unpredictable character, who when he wished could charm a bird off the proverbial tree, and yet at other times could be ruthless — nearly sadistic! By chance, being Mechanical Engineer Gorton, I had the opportunity to know him fairly well, as it was my regular job to meet him nearly every weekend at Chester and bring him by car to Gorton for the day. These car journeys were the occasions when he opened up and told me a good deal of what he wanted to do and why. All the time, however, he had at the back of his mind a determination to undermine Gresley's reputation.

'In my view Thompson was at his best when organising a department and thinking in terms of reducing costs; and he would have been a successful CME if only this resentment of Gresley had not been uppermost in his mind. He was a good picker of assistants, particularly where he knew he was weak — the control of staff and the handling of trade unions. He knew that his autocratic bearing irritated the latter before a discussion even started, and many is the time that one had to have another meeting after he had gone to straighten things out and smooth down ruffled feathers. I enjoyed working for E.T. although it was a precarious business. Some people just put a foot wrong once and they were "out". But those of us who were lucky enough *not* to be called by our Christian names lived through the exciting and sometimes depressing days.

'Thompson was a man who was very difficult to move if he had already made up his mind. I remember at one time he had an idea that all valve and piston, axlebox, and other 30,000-mile examinations should be carried out by the Workshops and not by the Motive Power Department. Having worked it out and got the joyful acceptance of the Motive Power Superintendents, he asked the General Manager, Sir Charles Newton, to come to Doncaster to hear about the plan and meet us all. The uproar amongst the Mechanical Engineers was such that it was said we were mutinous. I had the unenviable task of explaining to the GM that the whole scheme was unworkable, and I fully expected to be sacked the following day. Strange to say, nothing happened. It was the only occasion that I can recollect when E.T. was let down in public and did not bat an eyelid! I often wondered if there was something going on that I did not know about.'

Harrison says that Thompson spent an enormous amount on his clothes. He had over 50 suits, about 100 shirts, and very many pairs of shoes. He took great pride in his always immaculate appearance. But whilst most men disliked him, many women found him charming and those on his staff could generally get round him. Sometimes he displayed unexpected generosity. Once, for instance, on returning from London, he told Harrison that he had happened to call at Dunhill's and presented him with a pipe which had cost £7. And C. G. Gold writes:[7]

'To illustrate what a charming person the "Chief" could be, when he retired he gave a little private dinner party for his Assistant, Peppercorn, and his four Area Mechanical Engineers, namely Smeddle, Reeves, Harrison, and myself (who had been appointed by him Mechanical Engineer, Gorton Manchester). At this party he presented to each of us a miniature gold medallion of St Christopher, the patron saint of travellers.'

Harrison writes[8] that Thompson had a mind that was full of ideas, the majority of which was quite impracticable. He thinks that he probably pestered Gresley with many of them and that Gresley's abrupt rejection of these suggestions was another matter which embittered Thompson against him. Harrison adds that when Thompson told them to carry out some of his wilder ideas, they had to pretend acquiescence and hope that he would eventually forget all about them. Fortunately he generally did; but woe betide anyone who argued with him, or tried to point out the obvious difficulties. This only infuriated him and made him more determined than ever.

Peppercorn had an unhappy time as Thompson's Assistant. When he got home from work, he liked to have dinner and then settle down with a book. But he lived close to Thompson, who would frequently telephone him late in the evening and ask him to come round to discuss some problem.[9]

Thompson was intensely jealous of his position as CME. The episode of the *Bayonet* coach provides an example. The LNER was asked if the company could provide a special coach for the use of General Eisenhower, supreme commander designate of the invasion forces. This was agreed and the project was directed by Peppercorn, in consultation with an officer of Eisenhower's staff. A sleeping car was converted by stripping out several of the berths and installing office and living quarters. The body was armour plated against small arms fire and the completed coach was named *Bayonet*.[10] On 25 April 1945 Peppercorn received a nice letter from Sir Ronald Matthews, Chairman of the LNER, forwarding a very appreciative letter from General Eisenhower expressing his gratitude for his new *Bayonet* coach, and asking that his especial thanks should be extended to Thompson and Peppercorn. Thompson was very angry that Peppercorn should have been included in Eisenhower's letter, even though he had been primarily responsible for the coach's design.[11]

Thompson's first locomotive priority was to get rid of Gresley's conjugated valve gear. After he assumed office he lost no time in preparing for the directors a detailed record of all the locomotive failures which could be attributed to this gear, and told Sir Ronald Matthews the troubles experienced with it. As Gresley's engines were, in the opinion of the LNER Board, the finest in the country, Matthews found some difficulty in believing Thompson. However, the latter persisted and persuaded the chairman to agree to an independent opinion from an outside expert. He then approached Sir William Stanier[12] (who, incidentally, had built many three-cylinder engines for the LMS, but preferred three separate sets of valve gear for them). Stanier sent E. S. Cox, who submitted a report on the conjugated gear, showing that in run-down condition there was considerable lost motion on the middle valve and much trouble with hot inside big ends. The report was sent to the LNER over Stanier's signature[13] and Thompson used it to get the Board's approval for the construction of locomotives which differed widely from the Gresley pattern.

Thompson eventually decided on 10 standard locomotive classes. In addition to these a number of the existing classes were to be retained until the end of their useful lives, though some of them were to be rebuilt. All other classes in the LNER fleet were to be scrapped as soon as the existing stock of spare boilers had been used up. It was not a good plan. Harrison writes:[14] 'Except for the B1, all his thoughts turned to "Conversions". I had my fill of this at Gorton, because he could see what progress was being made. Had Gresley lived it is true to say that these conversions would never have been made. The locomotives would have been scrapped and no doubt H.N.G. would have enjoyed himself with new designs.' The Thompson plan is tabulated in outline below.

Class	Type	Duty	Remarks
A1	4-6-2	Express passenger	A prototype to be re-built from the existing A1 class Pacifics
A2	4-6-2	Heavy passenger and freight	A prototype to be rebuilt from the P2 2-8-2 class
B1	4-6-0	General utility	A new design using existing standard parts
K1	2-6-0	Mixed traffic	A prototype to be rebuilt from the K4 class 2-6-0
O1	2-8-0	Mineral	A prototype to be re-built from the Great Central O4 class 2-8-0
J11	0-6-0	Freight	A prototype to be re built from the GC 'Pom-Pom' 0-6-0 of Class J11
L1	2-6-4T	Mixed traffic tank	A new design
Q1	0-8-0T	Heavy shunting tank	A prototype rebuilt from the GC Q4 class 0-8-0
J50	0-6-0T	Medium shunting tank	A prototype rebuilt from the GN & LNE 0 6 0T of the same class number
		Light shunting tank	To be designed

It will be noticed that of the above 10 standard classes, no fewer than seven were rebuilds from existing locomotives. For his light shunting tank engine Thompson at first intended to keep the J72, which had been designed for the North Eastern Railway by Wilson Worsdell in 1898 as Class E1. The amusing sequel is that Peppercorn built 20 of these excellent little engines, starting in October 1950, and Harrison built eight more in 1951;[15] whereas most of Thompson's standard designs were dropped as soon as possible.

The classes which Thompson decided to retain were as follows:

Class	Type	Remarks
A10	4-6-2	Gresley's A1 Pacifics with a new class number. To be rebuilt as Class A3
A3	4-6-2	To be retained as built
A4	4-6-2	To be retained as built, but valances over the coupled wheels to be cut away
B17	4-6-0	The 'Sandringham' class. To be rebuilt with two cylinders and reclassified B2
D49	4-4-0	'Hunt' and 'Shire' classes. Experimental rebuilding to be undertaken. (A Class D two-cylinder 4-4-0 was planned in the light of experiment)
B16	4-6-0	NER mixed traffic. Valve gear to be modified
V2	2-6-2	To be retained as built
V1, V3	2-6-2T	To be retained as built
K3	2-6-0	To be rebuilt with two cylinders and reclassified K5

It will be noticed that amongst the engines to be scrapped were the 66 2-8-0s of Gresley's excellent three-cylinder O2 class. A proposal to rebuild the V1 and V3 2-6-2 tank classes with two cylinders was rejected in favour of the new L1 2-6-4 tank engine.

The history of these locomotive classes is narrated in the chapters which follow.

Notes

1 Peter Grafton *Edward Thompson of the LNER*; Kestrel Books, 1971, p45
2 B. C. Symes, letter to the author
3 ibid
4 Grafton, op cit, p46
5 R. C. Bond, conversation with the author
6 J. F. Harrison, letter to the author
7 C. G. Gold, letter to the author
8 J. F. Harrison, op cit
9 J. F. Harrison, conversation with the author
10 Grafton, op cit, pp108-109
11 Mrs Mather, conversation with the author
12 Cecil J. Allen; *The London & North Eastern Railway*; Ian Allan Ltd, 1966, p140
    O. S. Nock; *LNER Steam*; David & Charles, Pan Books edn, 1971, pp183-184
13 E. S. Cox, *Locomotive Panorama* vol I; Ian Allan Ltd, 1965, p140
14 J. F. Harrison, letter to the author
15 K. Hoole; *North Road Locomotive Works Darlington*; Roundhouse Books, 1967, pp62-63

Top: This photograph all too obviously illustrates the ugliness of the rebuilt No 4470 *Great Northern* (left) and A2/1 No 3697; both on Kings Cross shed on 11 May 1946. / *E. R. Wethersett*

Above: Great Northern in largely original condition, as running in 1929. The unhappy comparison with the Thompson rebuild is clear. / *E. R. Wethersett*

Right: Great Northern, as LNER No 113, is high above the River Tweed on the Royal Border Bridge with the up 'Flying Scotsman' in August 1947. Notice how the exhaust is clearing fairly well. / *E. R. Wethersett*

Right: Great things were expected of the L1 2-6-4Ts but they were not very successful, certainly not as compared with LMS and BR 2-6-4Ts. Westinghouse fitted No 67724 at Stratford in July 1948.
/ *E. R. Wethersett*

Below: A continuing life was foreseen by Thompson for the A4s and B17s. By 1951, the date of this photograph, the premier ER express, 'The Capitals Limited', is in the hands of A4 *Falcon* rather than a postwar Pacific and a B17, *Darlington*, is in command of an up Cambridge train rather than a B1.
/ *E. R. Wethersett*

7. Thompson's Only Design Memorial

In addition to the two V4 class 2-6-2 locomotives already running, 10 more had been ordered before Gresley's death. Thompson promptly cancelled them and in replacement built his B1 class two-cylinder 4-6-0s, with 6ft 2in coupled wheels instead of the V4's 5ft 8in.

It is likely that whenever Gresley enthusiasts discuss the great designer's engines the question will be raised as to whether the three-cylinder V4 would not, after all, have been a better general purpose engine than the two-cylinder B1. That the V4 was a very capable locomotive no one doubted, and indeed there was criticism in some quarters at the time that the engine which replaced it was not as strong. Nevertheless, there were strong reasons for not proceeding with the V4. It was expensive to build, its maintenance under wartime conditions would be comparatively difficult and costly, and the high-grade steels used in its construction were not readily available in 1942. In any case, J. F. Harrison, who knew both engines well, does not believe that the V4 would have handled the fast main line fitted goods as well as the B1.

The V4 was typical of Gresley's individualistic approach to a problem, and in this way he resembled G. J. Churchward of the Great Western. Churchward introduced a 2-6-0 with 5ft 8in wheels to replace 4-4-0 and other engines used on secondary services; Gresley provided a 2-6-2 with similar-sized wheels for the same purpose — both were conceptions new to British Railways at the time. Now the strange thing about Thompson's B1 is that it stemmed from a still earlier Churchward concept of 1903; for in that year there appeared on the Great Western a two-cylinder 4-6-0 No 98, the first of a long line of engines which eventually constituted the 'Saint' class and the first to have the free exhaust and long travel/long lap valves, which were to become a standard feature of all modern locomotives. After the development of his four-cylinder 'Star' class 4-6-0s, Churchward had intended that the 'Saints' should be the normal express engines, as they were better at getting away from stops than the four-cylinder 'Stars', but that the latter should be used for heavy non-stop trains running at high speed. In 1913, however, there was a change of policy, and it was decided that all future 4-6-0 engines should have four cylinders. The 'Saints', though, continued to perform excellent work on those main line services with frequent stops on which the 'Stars', with their ability to haul heavier loads over long distances at high speed, did not show to particular advantage. Churchward's successor, Collett, thought that they would be still more useful with more tractive effort, and in 1925 he reduced the driving wheels of No 2925 *Saint Martin* from 6ft 8½in to 6ft. The experiment was so successful that over 300 more 'Saints' with 6ft coupled wheels were built from 1928 onwards and given the new class name of 'Hall'. They gradually replaced all the surviving four-coupled passenger engines.

Stanier took the idea of the 4-6-0 engine with moderate sized coupled wheels to the London Midland & Scottish Railway, and his famous Class 5 4-6-0s were the result. These excellent engines handled a very large proportion of the LMS passenger and freight traffic, and were equally at home on express passenger and heavy goods trains. There were thus very good precedents for the adoption of a similar type of engine on the LNER (though one has a sneaking suspicion that Churchward himself would have preferred something more advanced than a modernised version of No 98).

The B1 performed every bit as well as the 'Hall' and the Class 5, though there was an obvious difference in its appearance. Both the GW and LMS engines had the shaped Belpaire firebox and coned boiler barrel that Churchward had designed to improve boiler circulation and reduce maintenance troubles. The B1 had the standard LNER parallel boiler with round-top firebox as fitted to the B17 and rebuilt B12 4-6-0s, though with the pressure raised from 200psi to 225. This was a well-tried and successful boiler which cost much less than the Churchward type. In any case, even had Thompson wished to do so, the middle of a war was a bad time to design and build a new and expensive boiler when there was a satisfactory type already available. Furthermore, the hard water (and absence of softening equipment) on the GC section resulted in the Belpaire fireboxes of the old Great Central engines being replaced so frequently that there was no saving from the theoretically lower maintenance costs of the Belpaire.[1]

In order to save expense in construction and in view of wartime shortages, parts were fabricated as far as possible and steel castings were used only for horn frames, wheel centres, and buffer sockets. Of their construction B. C. Symes writes:[2]

'The B1s were on the whole good, simple, "Go-anywhere" engines — until they got a bit run down and play developed in the axleboxes. One man told me that they then shook so badly that he mistook a yellow for a double yellow! I cannot say how far E. T. was responsible for their design, but I should say very little. I never saw any sketch or anything in writing, but of course he told the Chief Draughtsman what he wanted as regards main dimensions, weights per axle (which affected route availability), and specified that K2 cylinders and the Gresley three-bar crosshead were to be used. This of course meant that the K2 cylinders could not be used without alteration to the patterns. In fact new patterns were made, but there was no mention of this in the railway press. The footplate was thinner than usual so as to save material for the war effort. The wheels were existing patterns, but were of course new castings. As E. T. wanted to prove to the Civil Engineer that he could build a two-cylinder engine with no greater hammer blow than Gresley's three-cylinder B17, a special test was arranged on some bridge over which both types went at high speed. The test was all right, but only because E. T. had the reciprocating balance of the B1s fixed at 36% instead of the usual 40%. The boiler was a straightforward GN type, but with 225lb pressure, so naturally a bit heavier than usual. I think some existing flanging blocks were used for the plates.

'The B1 is recognisable as GN, or rather Doncaster, in most details, though a lot of it is due to a younger generation of thinking. The only obvious Darlington feature is the single downward curve of the footplate at the cab, in place of the GN "S" curve. As the man responsible for the drawings was ex-Darlington, this is not surprising. The practice of the various drawing offices largely died out and became LNER (with a Doncaster bias) when most of the men were transferred to the Central Drawing Office at Doncaster.'

Symes says that the reduction of the reciprocating balance was the main cause of the subsequent riding troubles, because a lightly-built engine is much more sensitive to out-of-balance forces than, say, a Pacific. In later years he had the job of rebalancing the engine to 40%. This was one of a number of jobs on various engines that his section was doing at the time. Once the drawings were issued to the Works, that was the end of the matter so far as the Drawing Office was concerned, and they did not necessarily hear what the results were. The Mechanical Inspectors of the CME's staff followed these things up, and if nothing more was heard in the Drawing Office they assumed that the alterations were satisfactory. However two other steps were taken to try and improve the bad riding, though Symes does not remember in what order they and the rebalancing were carried out. Firstly, the cab sides of all the engines were stiffened by fitting angle iron brackets from the sides to the frames to stop the vibration. Secondly, modifications were made to the valve setting to increase the lead from $\frac{1}{8}$in to $\frac{1}{4}$in to provide better cushioning for the pistons. This was a Darlington experiment and Symes does not know whether more than one engine was altered.

J. F. Harrison comments[3] that: 'Thompson intended to produce a general utility 4-6-0 like Stanier's Class 5 and very largely based on Stanier's design. This engine was to have a standard boiler which would be suitable for replacing the expensive boiler on the GC O4 mineral engines. As the B1, it was I believe a successful and useful engine, being as good as, if not better than, other constituent companies' mixed traffic 4-6-0s.' As regards round-top boilers, and Doncaster's preference for them, he remembers the Chief Draughtsman telling him that 'round-top boilers had the ability to flex without breaking crown stays.'

The B1 was fitted with a new type of bogie. Of this Harrison writes:[4]

'The Gresley bogie, being of the centre-pin type, allowed the engine (boiler and frame) to roll round the centre pin. [This was the bogie mentioned in Chapter 5 which appeared first on the D49 class and then superseded the swing link bogie on the Pacifics.]

'When Stanier came back from his visit to India to enquire into the derailment of Indian Pacifics, his report did in fact criticise the type of bogie Gresley was using. This had the effect of cautioning H. N. G. to think about different types of bogies. When Thompson came to power he naturally jumped at the idea of being able to show the world that even H. N. G.'s bogies were no good, and so he developed a side-bearer bogie based on (in fact copied from) the LMS bogie. You can imagine the effect this had on the Drawing Office staff, who were reluctant to change a satisfactory Gresley bogie; consequently the design characteristics were not properly worked out and the new bogies went into service with lightly-loaded helical side control springs and fairly light main bearing springs.'

As constructed, the Thompson bogie was adequate for the fairly light B1 4-6-0s; but much trouble arose when (as described later) it was fitted without alteration to the heavy Pacifics of both the Thompson and Peppercorn designs.

Construction of the first B1 4-6-0 started at Darlington in the year following Thompson's appointment as CME. On 8 July 1942 he gave orders that the new engine was to be built as quickly as possible, and, though there were wartime difficulties over labour and materials, it was completed on 19 December 1942[5]. Because its completion coincided with a visit to the United Kingdom by General Smuts, the Prime Minister of South Africa, the engine was named *Springbok*, and the immediately succeeding locomotives of the class were given names of different kinds of antelope. The principal dimensions of No 8301 *Springbok* were: cylinders 20in by 26in, diameter of coupled wheels 6ft 2in, boiler diameter 5ft 6in, grate area 27.9sq ft, boiler pressure 225psi, piston valve diameter 10in, maximum valve travel 6½in, steam lap 1⅝in.[6] The wheel diameter of 6ft 2in was 6in more than that of the V4, and the B1's weight of 71.1 tons was not much greater than the V4's 70.4 tons. With its smaller wheels and higher boiler pressure of 250psi the three-cylinder V4 had rather the greater tractive effort of 27,420lb, as compared with the B1's 26,878. The maximum axle load of the B1 was only 17¾ tons, so that it could work over most of the LNER system.

G. C. Gold was appointed Works Manager at Darlington North Road Works by Thompson in 1942, and was thus directly responsible for the construction of the first B1s. *Springbok* emerged from North Road Works painted in the austere wartime livery of unlined black and with the letters on the tender curtailed from LNER to NE. (One suspects that Darlington viewed this latter austerity with some satisfaction!). Gold relates the following incident in connection with the completion of the engine:[7]

'Thompson paid a visit to the works to have a look at his first designed locomotive, the Class B1 4-6-0 mixed traffic engine. He was accompanied by R. A. Smeddle, my immediate chief, who was responsible to

Thompson for North Road, Shildon Wagon Works, Faverdale Wagon Works, and Walkergate Works on Tyneside. Thompson was very pleased with the finished job and said to Smeddle: "I have decided we will equip this locomotive with discs on the lamp irons for daylight running and the usual lamps for the hours of darkness." The carrying of discs and lamps is a purely Operating Department function, to indicate to the signalman the class of train the locomotive is working. I had the temerity to ask if the Chief Operating Superintendent had been consulted. Thompson got angry. "I am the Chief Mechanical Engineer and *I* decide what will be fitted to *my* engines," he said in no uncertain terms: I then mentioned my doubts as to whether the disc to be used on the lamp bracket on top of the smokebox would clear the loading gauge. Thompson then got really angry and ordered a ladder to be placed in front of the smokebox. When he started to climb it Smeddle whispered to me: "Go on, follow him up. You have got your bloody self into this on your own and you can now get your bloody self out of it on your own." I followed Thompson up the ladder. He paused for a while at the top and then climbed down again, much to Smeddle's relief. Thompson then said to me: 'You have got a point there Gold; do it." We accordingly placed the lamp iron lower down on the smokebox door.

'The sequel to this was even funnier, because when the engine left the Works yard to go on trial the signalman on duty in the signalbox at the Works entrance refused to let it out because it was not carrying headlamps. Smeddle was very worried about the matter reaching the ears of Thompson, and, knowing of my Operating experience, asked me to go to the Superintendent's office at HQ York to try and get the matter sorted out. Luckily I knew the Chief Signalling Inspector and got him to alter the Appendix regulations to include this contingency. The matter, however, did not rest there, as the regular working of new locomotives on trial after they were run in was for them to work a passenger train from Darlington to Leeds via Harrogate and back. The engine was too large to turn on the LNER turntable at Leeds and had to run round the "triangle" which was on LMSR property, with the result that my friends at York HQ had to get agreement for the LMSR to alter their Appendix regulations as well, which they did. This took some time and Thompson never knew about it. Eventually the whole matter was dropped and the discs were never adopted.'

Building of the B1s continued for years after Thompson's retirement and there were eventually 410 of them. The first batch to be completed after the war were in LNER apple green livery, but those built under the British Railways regime were in the lined black livery of the old London & North Western Railway, which had been adopted for secondary passenger engines.

The B1 4-6-0 was one of the most useful engines ever possessed by the LNER, performing the same functions as Class 5 of the LMS, and, indeed, comparing well with the latter in the Interchange trials of 1948. Harrison regards the B1 as Thompson's 'only design memorial'.[8]

Notes
1   J. F. Harrison, letter to the author
2   B. C. Symes, letter to the author
3   Harrison, letter to the author
4   ibid
5   K. Hoole; *North Road Locomotive Works Darlington*; Roundhouse Books, 1967, pp54-55
6   Cecil J. Allen; *The London & North Eastern Railway*; Ian Allan Ltd, 1966, p140
7   G. C. Gold, letter to the author
8   Harrison, letter to the author

Top right: B1 class No 1005 *Bongo* with a down Cambridge train near New Southgate in 1946. / *E. R. Wethersett*

Centre right: B1 class No 61041 on the 'East Anglian' express in September 1949 passing Trowse Yard. / *E. Tuddenham*

Bottom right: B1 No 61409 in BR livery hard at work in the London suburbs on the GN main line. / *E. R. Wethersett*

EAST
ANGLIAN
Nº 61041
NORWICH

309
61409

Above right: In the early postwar years locomotive failures were all too common. Here B1 No 1112 is unusual substitute power for the up 'Yorkshire Pullman' threading the London suburbs on 11 October 1947. / *E. R. Wethersett*

Right: In Scotland the B1s were seldom used to their full capacity. No 61103 of Thornton comes off the Tay Bridge with a typical secondary train in 1950. / *E. R. Wethersett*

Below: Thompsons in double harness: Kings Cross' B1 No 61331 pilots L1 No 67744 near Marshmoor on a down Kings Cross outer suburban train in 1955. / *E. R. Wethersett*

8. The Thompson Pacifics

It is possible that no family of locomotives in the history of the London & North Eastern Railway were so unpopular with everybody who had anything to do with them as were the various classes of Pacifics designed by Edward Thompson. It is true that no fireman could love the big coal-eating 4-6-0 engines of the Great Central, but these solidly-built engines at least rode well and presented no problems in maintenance.

It is likely that Thompson, during his long embittered years as subordinate to Sir Nigel Gresley, had dreamed of designing big engines that would surpass his master's creations in both economy and efficiency. Furthermore, they would be clearly Thompson engines in both appearance and design and would incorporate as little as possible of Doncaster's traditional Great Northern practice. Gresley liked the drive of a three-cylinder engine to be on one axle; Thompson would have a divided drive. Gresley liked a derived motion for the inside cylinder; Thompson would have none of it. Gresley had built 2-8-2s and 2-6-2s; Thompson would replace both by Pacifics. Gresley's unstreamlined big engines had Great Northern chimneys; Thompson's would have stovepipes, and as far as possible the Great Northern 'S' curve of the running plate would go. If this seems unfair to Thompson it is in fact what happened, and it was not long after he became CME that he announced his plans for a Pacific with 6ft 2in coupled wheels which he intended should replace Gresley's

P2, or 'Cock o' the North', class 2-8-2s on the Edinburgh-Aberdeen run, the V2, or 'Green Arrow', class 2-6-2s on express freight trains, and also the Great Central B7 four-cylinder mixed traffic 4-6-0s, the North Eastern B16 three-cylinder mixed traffic 4-6-0s, and the Great Northern type K3 three-cylinder 2-6-0s on the heavier express freight train duties. Both the P2 and V2 classes had the 6ft 2in, coupled wheels which Thompson had selected for his Pacific, whilst the other three classes had 5ft 7in or 5ft 8in coupled wheels.

Thompson decided to produce prototypes for his mixed traffic Pacific class by rebuilding the P2s. There seems little doubt, in the light of another rebuilding to be mentioned later, that he relished the opportunity of destroying such notable examples of Gresley's work. These fine engines did have faults, which have already been mentioned. But they would have been invaluable in the haulage of the heavy wartime traffic over the far easier curves of the LNER Kings Cross-Newcastle main line. If improved performance in Scotland had been sought, it could have been found in a comparatively minor rebuilding with an Italian bissel bogie replacing the leading coupled axle and pony truck, as proposed by Chapelon and Pennoyer. On the other hand, if they had been moved to England they could have been made quite satisfactory by replacing the swing-link pony trucks by others having spring side control. Gresley had already done this in respect of the Pacifics' bogies, and the V2s' pony trucks were thus altered a few years later. One of the great assets of these engines was, of course, the adhesion provided by their eight coupled wheels. On conversion to Pacifics the only advantage they would have over an A4 on the Aberdeen main line would be the rather greater tractive effort conferred by their smaller wheels (40,318lb as compared with the A4's 35,455). It was unlikely, therefore, that they would be able to haul any heavier trains than the A4, and to that extent their conversion was a waste of money.

However, to return to Thompson's project: the power required from his Pacific would, he considered, require more than two cylinders.

He chose three, rather than four, following the traditions of Doncaster and Darlington rather than that of Gorton. He decided on an inside Walschaerts valve gear for the middle cylinder, in place of Gresley's conjugated gear. This entailed either a divided drive or driving on the leading coupled axle. Thompson selected the former. Whilst he was at Stratford the B17 4-6-0s had suffered trouble with the inside-cylinder big end. These engines had a divided drive and connecting rods of unequal length, and Thompson deduced that connecting rods for outside and inside cylinders should be of equal length.[1]

In obtaining authority to carry out the rebuilding of the P2s, Thompson had assured the Chief General Manager of the LNER that he would make full use of existing parts. This led to the retention of the original rather short connecting rods which, on the P2s, drove on to the second of the four coupled axles from cylinders positioned between the pony truck and the leading coupled axle. In relation to the smokebox, this was the same position as that of the Pacifics' cylinders. But as Thompson wanted the outside cylinders to drive on the second coupled axle (the original third axle of the P2 class) they had to be sited immediately in front of the leading coupled axle (the original second axle). G. J. Churchward's arrangement of the outside cylinders on his four-cylinder engines had been similar; but these had a diameter sufficiently small to be mounted outside the trailing bogie wheels. The outside cylinders of a three-cylinder engine of this power were of too great a diameter to be so placed within the loading gauge. Thompson therefore had to place the bogie sufficiently far forward for its trailing wheels to be in front of the cylinders. A draughtsman remarked of the result that one could almost say that the rebuilds were designed round the connecting rods![2] Troubles from this arrangement ruined any chance the engines might have had of being a success. Thompson insisted that the live steam pipes connecting the superheater header to the cylinders should be as short as possible, though as Churchward's designs had shown, this was quite unnecessary. As the cylinders were so far back the boiler had to be shortened to give the short steam pipes sufficient clearance, and this resulted in an unusually lengthy smokebox. The exhaust steam pipes from the outside cylinders ran along the outside of the frames immediately below the running plate.

The original P2 boilers were retained, but were shortened as stated above and the pressure was increased from 220 to 225psi. The Gresley banjo-shaped dome casing was retained and the perforated steam collector that it housed, in spite of Thompson's dislike of this fitting, because of his undertaking to use existing parts. The double Kylchap exhaust was also retained, but the double chimney was plain with straight sides and was flanked by small wing-type smoke deflectors (which proved singularly ineffective). The use of three independent sets of valve gear allowed the maximum cut-off to be increased from 65 to 75%, with a maximum valve travel of 6¾in. It also allowed the piston valves to be more conveniently placed so that their diameter could be increased from 9in to 10in. The bogie was the pattern which had been designed for the B1 4-6-0s.

No 2005 *Thane of Fife* was rebuilt first and appeared in its new guise on 16 January 1943. On 2 April it was back in service on the Edinburgh-Aberdeen main line, followed by the other five engines as they were completed during 1943 and 1944.[3] In 1945 the class was designated A2/2.

In their rebuilt form the engines looked ungainly, and the troubles experienced with them matched their appearance. T. C. B. Miller says that the frames flexed up to about 3in.[4] J. F. Harrison comments[5] that 'short connectng rods, for a start, are not good (as shown by the Raven Pacifics), and between the cylinders and the six-coupled wheels there developed a serious frame weakness'. The flexing was partly due to the inside cylinder being sited where on the Gresley Pacifics there was a frame bracing member.[6] Over a certain range of speed there was 'nosing'. On one occasion the Chief Draughtsman went out on a Thompson Pacific and returned terrified at the experience.[7] The shed master at

Peterborough reported of a later batch of Thompson mixed traffic Pacifics that the riding was very bad and that they were troublesome to maintain.[8] The higher power to weight ratio resulting from the reduction in the adhesive weight and the lowering of the factor of adhesion from 4.06 to 3.67 made the engines very prone to slipping and reduced their haulage capacity.[9]

During 1945 No 2005 made eight visits to Cowlairs Works. The principal troubles were cylinders working loose, exhaust steam pipes breaking, live steam pipes being torn away from the header in the smokebox, and the bolts breaking between the smokebox and the saddle.[10] All these faults were due to the flexing of the frames ahead of the outside cylinders. The rough riding was mainly due to the bogie side control springs being too weak, though this was not discovered until after the appearance of Peppercorn's Pacifics. Whilst the bogies were adequate for the comparatively light B1s, they were quite unsuitable for heavy Pacifics.

In an attempt at curing the flexing of the frames, stiffening plates, one inch thick, were bolted to the inside of the frames to strengthen the portion between the inside cylinder casting and the frame stay near the outside cylinders. To give flexibility to the exhaust steam pipes, they were divided into two sections connected by an expansion joint near the cylinder steam chest. The live steam pipes were lengthened and given wide sweeping curves to absorb any movement on expansion. (These modifications were later applied to all other Thompson Pacifics.)

Before the rebuilding of the P2s had been completed, Thompson had already earmarked another Gresley design for 'improvement' into a similar type of mixed traffic Pacific. In January 1943 a Pacific version of a V2 2-6-2 was planned, with the same type of front end as the rebuilt P2s. The last four of a batch of V2s on order were therefore turned out from Darlington during 1944-45 as Pacifics. The coupled wheelbase was shorter than that of the V2s — a necessity if the front end was to be standardised with that of the A2/2s — but they had as an addition rocking grates and hopper ashpans

— the first LNER engines to be so fitted. The V2 boiler and V2 rear end were retained, though the working pressure was increased from 220 to 225psi. The diameter of the cylinders was increased by $\frac{1}{2}$in. The bogies were the same as those of the A2/2s. The Gresley banjo dome with perforated steam collector was retained and, like the A2/2s, the engines had the Kylchap double exhaust and plain double chimneys with small wing-type smoke deflectors. The Great Central type of regulator handle was fitted at first, but this proved unpopular and was replaced by the Gresley pull-out handle at the first heavy overhaul. The four engines were classified A2/1. As might be expected, they suffered from the same troubles as the A2/2s. The V2s were, as T. C. B. Miller says, very good rugged engines. The Thompson replacement did not compare with them.

One of Thompson's earliest actions on becoming CME was to prepare for the LNER Directors a list of all the failures of Gresley engines that he could trace, particularly those which could be attributed to the conjugated valve gear. Now that Thompson had some of his own Pacifics in operation, the Chief General Manager asked him what improvements had been effected under his direction, including reductions in the consumption of coal.[11] This enquiry led to some trials between an A4, an A2/2, and an A2/1, which were held during January 1945. The engines concerned were A4 No 2512 *Silver Fox* (at that time fitted with a single blast pipe and chimney), A2/2 No 2003 *Lord President*, and A2/1 No 3697 (later *Duke of Rothesay*). The trials were carried out with both express passenger and express goods trains. Owing to mechanical failures on the A4 and the A2/1, the only worthwhile comparison was on the 10.30am Kings Cross-Leeds express. On this *Silver Fox* consumed 52.3lb of coal per mile, *Lord President* 70.5lb, and No 3697 69lb. Weather conditions, however, were poor. Further tests were made during the following April and far better figures were obtained. The passenger trains were heavy, usually of 17 or 18 coaches, and the goods trains varied between 54 and 61 wagons weighing 505 to 706 tons. This time coal consumption on the three engines was fairly equal, with, as one would expect, the A4 showing best on the passenger trains, whilst the A2s, with their smaller coupled wheels, consumed less coal and had a better acceleration on the goods trains. *Silver Fox* burned 38lb of coal per mile on the passenger trains, *Lord President* 42.73, and No 3697 41.69. On the goods trains *Silver Fox* burned 45.7lb, *Lord President* 40.89, and No 3697 36.75. That the A2/2 had a consistently higher coal consumption than the A2/1 was probably due to its larger firebox. The tests showed, however, that Thompson had not reduced coal consumption at all, and it is unfortunate that his reply to the Chief General Manager does not appear to have survived.

Thompson, at any rate, was satisfied enough with his Pacifics to order his standard A2 class (later designated A2/3), which were in all major respects identical with his reconstruction of the P2s. The 1945 Locomotive Construction Programme authorised 30 of these entirely new engines. The only significant changes from the A2/2 class were an increase in the boiler pressure to 250psi and a reduction in the cylinder diameter from 20in to 19in. In October 1945 another 13 were ordered for the 1946 programme. In fact, however, only 15 of the A2/3s were ever built.

Before the first of the A2/3s appeared, however, Thompson had provided another example of his hatred of Gresley. His plan to rebuild as the prototype for a new express locomotive one of Gresley's A1 Pacifics was mentioned in Chapter 6. In July and August 1944 two sketches were produced showing different arrangements of a Gresley Pacific rebuilt with three sets of Walschaerts valve gear and divided drive. In one of these the outside cylinders remained in the existing position between the bogie wheels, whilst the inside cylinder was further forward above the leading bogie axle, the inside and outside connecting rods being of different lengths. In the other drawing the cylinder layout and front end arrangement was the same as that adopted for the A2 Pacifics. The boiler in both drawings was that fitted to the A4 class. Both showed the ugly feature of cab sides cut short and both omitted the graceful GN 'S' curves. The A2 pattern of straight double chimney and wing deflector plates were also included in both drawings. The second drawing was, as one would expect, chosen by Thompson, but the small deflector plates were omitted as they were not proving effective in practice.[12]

At the time that Thompson's plans for rebuilding an A1 were approved, there were 18 of these engines which had not yet been rebuilt as A3: No 4470 *Great Northern*, 4472 *Flying Scotsman*, 4475 *Flying Fox*, 4476 *Royal Lancer*, 4481 *St Simon*, 2543 *Melton*, 2546 *Donovan*, 2547 *Doncaster*, 2548 *Galtee More*, 2550 *Blink Bonny*, 2556 *Ormonde*, 2557 *Blair Atholl*, 2562 *Isinglass*, 2564 *Knight of Thistle*, 2565 *Merry Hampton*, 2567 *Sir Visto*, 2569 *Gladiateur*, and 2572 *St Gatien*. All these had, of course, been modified since their original construction to have long travel and long lap valves and were extremely good engines. Out of all of them, to the horror of everybody who had been connected with Doncaster, Thompson selected the pioneer of the class and one of the only two to have borne the initials GNR on its tender, No 4470 (originally 1470) *Great Northern*. Of this action, J. F. Harrison writes[13]:

'All the time Thompson had at the back of his mind a determination to undermine Gresley's reputation, and what better way than to take the first Pacific that Gresley built, and rebuild it, eliminating the conjugated valve gear. The conjugated valve gear was not suitable if it was not properly maintained, and during the war years maintenance in all respects had been sadly neglected. I believe Gresley himself would have given it up for this reason, and I like to think that he would have adopted the Caprotti gear which I fitted to the last Pacific built in this country, the BR Class 8 No 71000 *Duke of Gloucester*. The Board agreed to the conversion of *Great Northern*, although all of us tried hard to persuade Thompson to take any Pacific except the first; but he would have none of it!'

As Thompson wanted his new Pacific to be Class A1 (it was later designated A1/1), all the 17 remaining Gresley A1s became Class

A10 from April 1945. The new *Great Northern* was completed in September 1945. It was indeed new because the old engine had been destroyed except for the wheel centres and some of the axles.[14] In fact, the construction of this new Pacific was something of a 'wangle' because, owing to a shortage of steel the Ministry of Supply would authorise major repairs of locomotives but not new construction. It was therefore as a 'major repair' that an entirely new engine was built round old wheel centres and axles! Some concession was made to Thompson's agreement to make use of all serviceable parts, because the frames of the old *Great Northern*, which only dated from May 1933, were used again for Class A3 Pacific No 2573 *Harvester*.[15]

It is curious that C. B. Collett of the Great Western exhibited the same spite against a disliked predecessor by destroying G. J. Churchward's *The Great Bear* and building a 'Castle' class engine in its place as a nominal 'reconstruction'. There was, in fact, something of an affinity between Churchward's and Gresley's engines. Churchward was handicapped in his testing of *The Great Bear* by it being limited to the Paddington-Bristol main line owing to its heavy axle loading. Testing of the engine was badly held up by World War I, and when tests were renewed after it, Churchward would have appreciated the opportunity to try his engine on another main line. When he heard that Gresley was building a Pacific he remarked that 'Gresley could have had our "Bear" to play with if only we had known in time.'[16] Both companies would probably have gained valuable information. Gresley might have adopted long-travel valves from the start and the exchange between his Pacifics and the Great Western 'Castles' would probably never have taken place.

Practically all the features of the A2 Pacifics were repeated in Thompson's *Great Northern*, producing the same weaknesses, and whilst the expansion joints in the exhaust steam pipes stopped them breaking, it was impossible to keep the joints tight so that there was considerable leakage of the exhaust steam.[17] The A1/1 had the A4 boiler and double Kylchap exhaust and chimney. The latter was the same plain type, but was slightly improved in appearance by the addition of a half-round beading to the rim; all Thompson and Peppercorn Pacifics were fitted with this type of double chimney until 1949, when it was replaced by a much more handsome lipped chimney. A memento of Thompson's time at Stratford was the Great Eastern blue in which his A1/1 was painted, embellished with double red lines, and his pre-Grouping allegiance was commemorated by the letters NE, which appeared on the tender sides.[18] These two letters were in theory a wartime economy in place of the full LNER, but it was hardly convincing when matched with the expensive livery of this engine. In May 1947, at its first general repair, *Great Northern* was repainted in the standard green livery with full lettering.

The cab layout proved most unpleasant. It was difficult to climb into the cab and it swayed about at speed, probably due to inadequate staying. On 24 November the engine was returned to Doncaster for modification and the opportunity was seized to deepen the cab sides and restore the normal shape of the running plate at the rear end with the flat 'S' curve. Large smoke deflectors were fitted at the same time.

Before these modifications were carried out, coal consumption trials were held between *Great Northern* and A4 class Pacific No 4466 *Sir Ralph Wedgwood*. Both engines hauled trains of about 475 tons between Kings Cross and Grantham and returned almost identical figures of coal consumed.[19]

Thompson intended to rebuild all the remaining A10 class Pacifics in the same fashion; and in October 1945 authority was obtained to build 16 completely new similar locomotives in the 1946 Locomotive Construction Programme. However, before they could be put in hand Thompson had been succeeded by Peppercorn and the eventual A1s were vastly different engines.[20]

The first of Thompson's standard A2 class, No 500, was completed at Doncaster in May 1946 the two thousandth engine to be built at Doncaster Works since construction began there in 1867. At a ceremony at Marylebone station on 29 May it was named *Edward Thompson* after the now retiring CME, for his term of office expired on 30 June 1946.

No 500 had the same basic layout as the rebuilt P2s. The boiler barrel was the same length, but the combustion chamber was a little longer and the smokebox a little shorter to compensate. Other features included electric lighting, self-cleaning smokebox, and a hopper ashpan. Later a rocker grate was fitted. To the onlooker, the most noticeable differences from the A2/2 was the round dome in place of the banjo type, the large smoke deflectors instead of the small wing pattern, and the half-round beading on the rim of the double chimney. The bogie was slightly modified, and the last of the 15, No 524, had a bogie with helical bearing springs instead of the Thompson pattern of laminated springs.[21]

The A2/3s suffered from the same troubles as beset the other Thompson Pacifics; the cylinders worked loose, saddle bolts sheared, and the riding was rough. The middle eccentric needed frequent lubrication by the engine crews, but the long stretch to the oil containers tempted men to neglect it, and the Thompson gear, therefore, showed no maintenance improvement over Gresley's conjugated motion.[22]

On 7 August 1946 Peppercorn ordered comparative trials between No 500 and a V2 to see how they compared in coal consumption and in capacity — a necessary test, because the A2/3 was intended primarily to replace the V2. The trials were handicapped by bad coal, and the consumption of this was about the same in the two engines; but the report stressed the superiority of the A2/3's double Kylchap exhaust over the single blastpipe of the V2. Nevertheless, the conclusion was that it would be wasteful in coal, water, and engine power to use the A2/3s on relatively light duty, and that their greater capacity could only be justified on the very heaviest work.[23]

The history of all these Thompson Pacifics in traffic is of some depressing interest. The rebuilt P2s — that is, the A2/2s — returned to the Edinburgh-Aberdeen main line, but it was soon found that owing to their lack of adhesion the heaviest load that they could manage was about 500 tons, as opposed to the 550 tons tare that the engines were rostered to haul before rebuilding. As the A3 Pacifics had been rostered to work 480 tons northbound and 420 southbound, and as 500 tons was well within the capacity of the A4s, it was clear that the engines could no longer fulfil the purpose for which they had been designed, and that not only the cost of rebuilding them, but also part of their original cost had been wasted. In fact the A4s, as far as possible, were used to haul the heaviest trains and by the beginning of 1946 the A2/2s had been practically taken off passenger trains and were working express goods, fish, and parcels trains.[24] When the Peppercorn Pacifics began to appear, the A2/2s were transferred to England, three going to York and the other three to New England. Here they were employed on express goods together with some haulage of passenger trains.[25]

Mileage between general repairs was poor, and in March 1947, whilst still in Scotland, five out of the six were laid up in the Cowlairs Works at the same time. (In the same month three out of the four A2/1s were laid up at Darlington.)[26]

There was nothing wrong with the steam circuit of the engines, which were remarkably free running. Cecil J. Allen records[27] a run from Darlington to York with No 60502 *Earl Marischal* hauling six coaches weighing 220 tons gross, during which the speed from Thirsk onwards was as high as he had ever known by a LNER Pacific, if not higher, and almost certainly the highest with 6ft 2in coupled wheels on level track: the 4.2 miles from Thirsk to Sessay were covered at 92-92½mph. Allen was not on the train himself and did not know what conditions were like on the footplate, but these engines were unpopular owing to their tendency to roll at speed.[28]

The V2 replacements, the four A2/1s, all went for a short time to the North East area, where they were used on slow passenger trains and a few express passenger and fast goods workings. In November 1944 two of them were despatched to Kings Cross, where they joined the other Pacifics on express passenger and fast goods trains The Kings Cross men disliked them because of their rough riding, their steam reversers (which were soon removed) and the continual leakage from the expansion joints of the outside cylinder exhaust pipes. The other two went to the Haymarket shed in Scotland, where they were equally unpopular and were never used on the principal expresses, to which the A4s were generally allocated. The A2/1s were generally employed on secondary express passenger and express goods trains. These four engines were probably the worst of Thompson's Pacifics.

The rebuilt *Great Northern* went to Kings Cross in October 1945, and worked in the same link as the other Pacifics there. Kings Cross put up with it till June 1950, and then got rid of it to New England, where it ran mostly on semi-fast passenger, parcels, and fast goods trains. In September 1951 it was at Grantham and was tried for a time in that depot's top link with two regular drivers, but it was so unreliable that it was withdrawn from regular duties and became the spare engine.[29] Thus Thompson's only Pacific designed exclusively for express passenger duties had the melancholy distinction of being far worse than the very first Doncaster Pacific built 23 years before.

Of the 15 A2/3 Pacifics, 10 went to the North Eastern area, five to the Southern area, and one to Scotland. At that time many of the Gresley Pacifics were badly run down due to lack of maintenance during the war, so Kings Cross used the A2/3s for a time on nominal main-line express duties. But as soon as the Peppercorn Pacifics became available, Kings Cross got rid of them and they went to New England, where they were employed on the same duties as other Thompson Pacifics. In the North Eastern area they worked many of the main-line express passenger and fast goods trains.[30] One of them, No 60524 *Herringbone*, it is only fair to say, performed what Cecil J. Allen described as 'the most astonishing run that I have ever known in the northbound direction between York and Darlington.' With an 11-coach train of 380 tons gross, the speed beyond Thirsk soon reached 90mph on the dead level and 41 miles were covered at an average of 82.5mph.[31] But the ability of Thompson's Pacifics to run fast was never in doubt; it was primarily as vehicles that they failed.

In a letter to the author, K. R. M. Cameron writes: 'The riding of the [Peppercorn] A1 and A2 locomotives did not strike me as in any way rough or dangerous, but I cannot say the same for those Thompson monstrosities, the A2/1, A2/2 and A2/3. These engines, with their longer wheelbase, developed quite an alarming "yawing" motion which at times could be quite disconcerting, especially to those of us who did not ride on them very frequently.'

The principal dimensions of the various Thompson Pacifics were as follows:

	A2/2	A2/1	A2/3	A1/1
Cylinders (3)	20in × 26in	19in × 26in	19in × 26in	19in × 26in
Heating Surface, sq ft				
Firebox	237	215	245.3	231.2
Tubes	1,211.57	1,211.57	1,211.57	1,281.4
Flues	1,004.5	1,004.5	1,004.5	1,063.7
Superheater	679.67	679.67	679.67	748.9
Total	3,132.74	3,110.74	3,141.04	3,325.2
Grate Area, sq ft	50	41.25	50	41.25
Boiler Pressure, psi	225	225	250	250
Coupled Wheels	6ft 2in	6ft 2in	6ft 2in	6ft 8in
Tractive effort, lb	40,318	36,387	40,430	37,347
Weight, Engine	101T 10C	98T	101T 10C	101T 10C
Adhesive Weight	66T	66T	66T	66T
Max Axle Load	22T	22T	22T	22T
Engine Wheel Base	36ft 11in	36ft 8in	36ft 11in	38ft 5in

The numbering of these engines was a little complex because Thompson's renumbering scheme was being put into effect while they were being built. In 1943 a scheme was prepared by which blocks of numbers would be allotted to various locomotive types: 1-999 being allocated, for instance, to the largest express passenger tender engines and 1000-1999 to six-coupled passenger and mixed traffic tender engines. Action on the scheme began on 13 January 1946 and was completed on 18 January 1947. The numbers eventually given to the Pacifics within the allotted blocks differed from the original plan. It will suffice to say that the A4s were numbered 1-34, the A3s and A10s 35-112, Thompson's rebuilt *Great Northern* became 113, the first of the A2/3s was numbered 500, the A2/2s were 501-6, the A2/1s 507-10, and the remaining A2/3s 511-24.

It is not easy to make a definite assessment of Thompson's Pacifics. It is clear that they were fast and free-running, bad riders, mechanically faulty in various respects and thoroughly unreliable. Doncaster drawing office undoubtedly produced an excellent steam circuit, but it would seem that they were too hampered by the mechanical layout on which Thompson insisted to be able to make good engines of them. The result was that their riding was generally rough and at times even dangerous at high speed, and their design weaknesses led to much time off the road and high maintenance costs. On the whole, therefore, they must rank with such famous locomotive failures (though for entirely different reasons) as Webb's compounds for the London & North Western Railway, Dugald Drummond's 4-6-0s for the London & South Western and E. A. Watson's 400 class 4-6-0 engines for the Great Southern & Western.

Below: A2/2 class Pacific No 2005 *Thane of Fife,* rebuilt from P2 class 2-8-2. / *LPC*

Notes

1 Peter Grafton; *Edward Thompson of the LNER*; Kestrel Books, 1971, pp72-73
2 The Railway Correspondence & Travel Society, *Locomotives of the LNER*, Part 2A, p143
3 ibid, pp143f
4 T. C. B. Miller, conversation with the author
5 J. F. Harrison, letter to the author
6 Grafton, op cit, p103
7 G. W. Carpenter, information to the author
8 ibid
9 Grafton, op cit, p63
   Cecil J. Allen; *British Pacific Locomotives*; Ian Allan Ltd, 1962, pp94f
10 RCTS, op cit, pp143f
   Carpenter, information to the author
11 Allen, op cit, pp100f
12 RCTS, op cit, pp174f
13 J. F. Harrison, letter to the author
14 Grafton, op cit, p91
15 RCTS, op cit, pp174f
16 Colonel H. C. B. Rogers; *G. J. Churchward*; Allen & Unwin, 1974, pp128-130
17 Grafton, op cit, pp90-93
18 RCTS, op cit, pp174f
19 ibid
20 ibid
21 ibid, pp164f
22 Grafton, op cit, p103
23 RCTS, op cit, pp164f
24 ibid, pp143f
25 ibid
26 ibid, pp143f, 156f
27 Allen, op cit, pp94f
28 RCTS, op cit, pp143f
29 ibid, pp174f
30 ibid, pp164f
31 Allen, op cit, p102

Above: A2/2 No 60506 *Wolf of Badenoch* leaving Inverkeithing with the 2.15pm Edinburgh to Aberdeen train 1949. / *E. R. Wethersett*

Left: A2/2 No 60503 *Lord President* at Newcastle in February 1958 after arrival from York. Note lipped chimney. / *I. W. Coulson*

3697
3697

DUKE OF ROTHESAY
508
L N E R

Left: A2/1 class Pacific No 3697, later named *Duke of Rothesay.* The Pacific version of the V2.
/ *E. R. Wethersett*

Below left: A2/1 class Pacific No 508 *Duke of Rothesay* as later modified with large smoke deflectors.
/ *Ian Allan Library*

Right: A2/3 class Pacific No 60511 *Airborne* at Prestonpans on an up freight: large deflectors, stovepipe chimney, double Kylchap exhaust.
/ *E. R. Wethersett*

Below: A2/3 No 60524 *Herringbone* at Motherwell on a Carlisle to Perth parcels train on the night of 9 November 1963. / *N. Pollock*

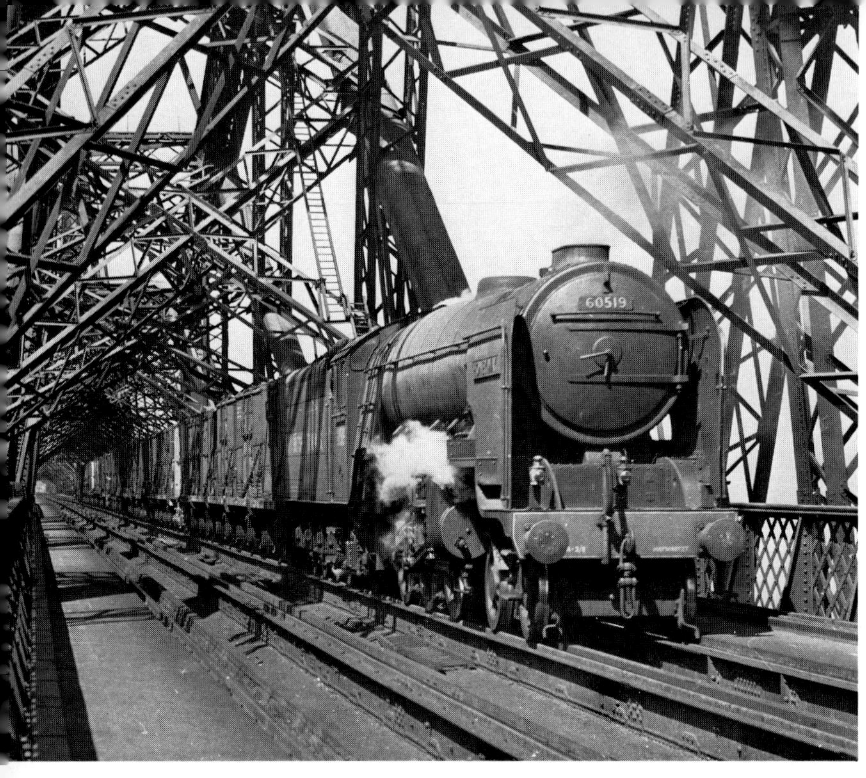

Left: A2/3 No 60519 *Honeyway* on an up fish train on the Forth Bridge in August 1949. / *E. R. Wethersett*

Below: The first Pacific, No 4470 *Great Northern*, rebuilt as A1/1, lettered 'NE' and painted royal blue.

Bottom: No 60113 *Great Northern* with improved lines at cab and firebox, lipped chimney and large deflector plates emblazoned with the Great Northern Railway armorial achievement. The train is the Northern Rubber Co Festival special seen at Potters Bar. / *E. R. Wethersett*

Right: A fine study of No 500 *Edward Thompson*, at Doncaster in September 1946. / *E. R. Wethersett*

Below right: *Edward Thompson* in service, passing Stoke box with a very clear exhaust at the head of a 13-coach Newcastle express in July 1951. / *E. R. Wethersett*

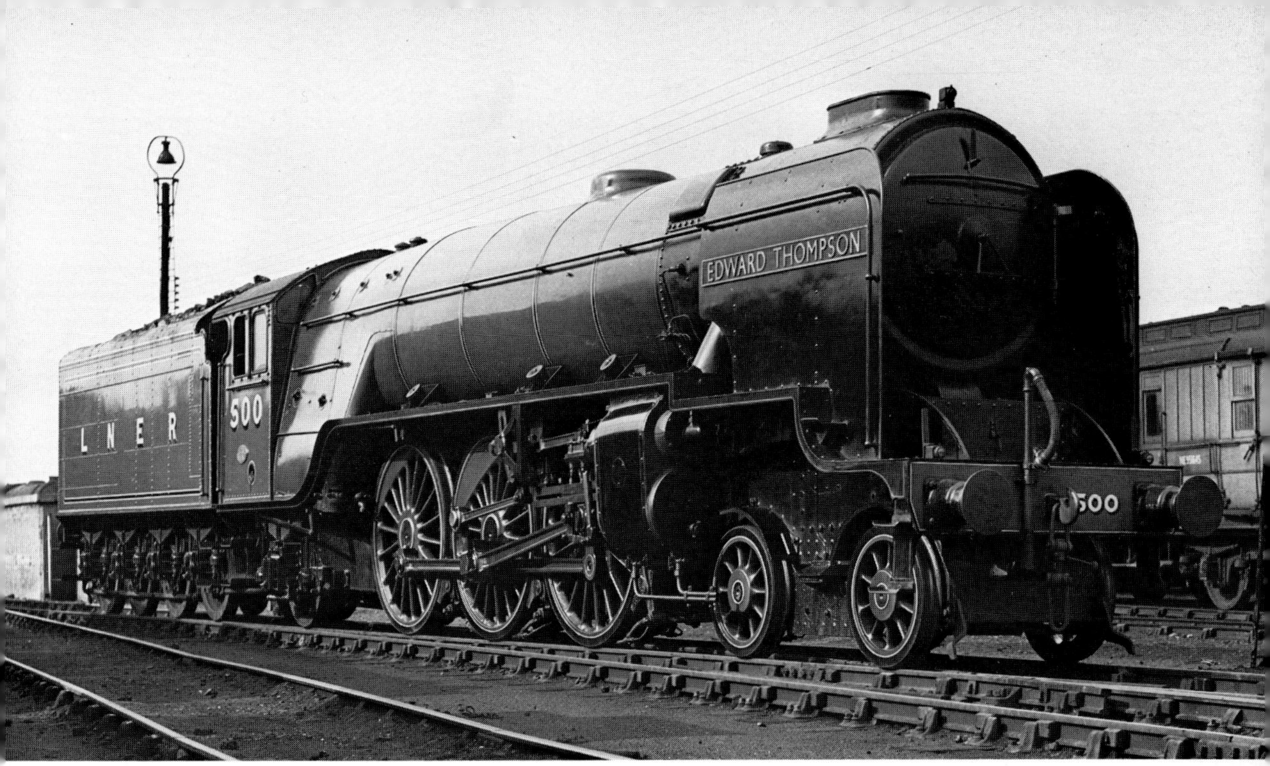
EDWARD THOMPSON
500
L N E R
500

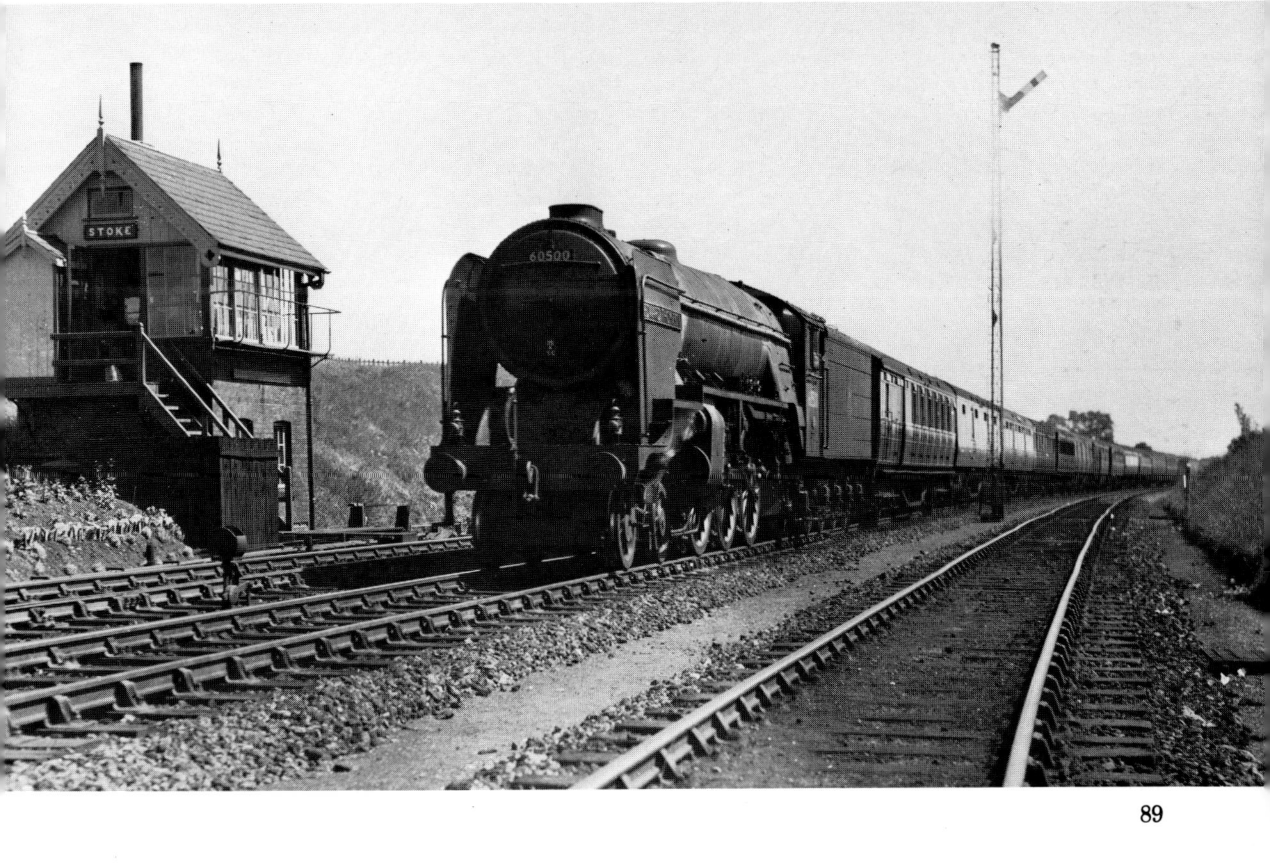
STOKE
60500

9. Thompson's Other Engines

Late in 1947 a 'Route Availability' scheme, which had been introduced in 1940 by the Southern Area Civil Engineer's department, was adopted for general use throughout the LNER. There were nine categories of route which were given RA numbers from 1 to 9, RA1 being the most restrictive and RA9 suitable for the heaviest engines. From September 1947 the RA number was painted on the cab sides of all engines. The method of calculating this number was a little complicated. The principal factor was axle load, but an engine with a very short wheelbase, and hence with its weight distributed over a very short distance, might be allotted a higher RA number than its axle loading would suggest. Any locomotive having an RA number equal to or less than that of a route could work over that route provided it was not barred by either exceeding the loading gauge or having too long a rigid wheelbase, in the case of a route having low bridges or tunnels, or unusually sharp curves. On the other hand, if a route had no bridge spans over a certain length, some engines with a higher RA number than that of the route might be allowed over it.[1]

In designing an engine for general use over a railway system, it is generally necessary to strike a balance between getting the greatest possible power and the ability to run over the greatest possible route mileage. A study of LNER routes showed that a figure of RA5 would allow an engine to run over all save a few short branches and some longer lines carrying a very light traffic. This represented a maximum axle loading of approximately 18 tons. Of course, at the time that Thompson was selecting his standard engines, the RA system had not been adopted but the route restrictions were approximately the same. Thus when Thompson decided on an engine for general goods work, able to run over most of the system, it was apparent that the axle loading must not exceed 18 tons. In addition, it would have to be a 0-6-0 because certain turntables, particularly in Scotland, would not take anything longer. The J39s were ruled out because they had an axle load of about 19 tons. However, the 5ft 2in coupled wheels of the J39s had proved suitable for the type of work envisaged. Gresley, recognising the need, would probably have designed a new engine for the job. Rather than do this, Thompson always preferred to rebuild an existing class, even though in some of his rebuilds there was very little left of the original engines.

Of existing 0-6-0s, there were only two classes which met the requirement — the J6, built for the Great Northern, and the J11 of the Great Central.

The first series of the locomotives which were subsequently classifid J6 by the LNER consisted of 15 built for the GNR by H. A. Ivatt in 1911. Gresley continued building them with slight modifications up till the end of the GNR's separate existence in 1922, by which time there were 110 in the class. All the J6s were superheated and had 19in by 26in cylinders with 8in piston valves operated by Stephenson gear. The boiler diameter was 4ft 8in and the maximum axle load 18 tons. They were efficient engines and very popular with their crews. They were used on all types of duty: express goods, coal, general freight, and semi-fast passenger trains. On the latter they could run at well over 60mph, and were preferred by their drivers to the J2 0-6-0s, which had 5ft 8in wheels, probably because the latter with their higher-pitched boilers were somewhat unsteady when running fast.[2]

The J11 class 0-6-0s were the first engines built under the regime of J. G. Robinson for the Great Central. The first appeared in 1901 and construction continued till 1910, when they numbered 174. Because their sharp exhaust was likened to the noise made by the one-pounder automatic 'pom-pom' gun used by the Boers in the war then in progress the engines were nicknamed 'Pom-Poms' by the footplatemen. They originally had saturated boilers and 18½in by 26in cylinders with slide valves. Superheating of the whole class began in 1913, but was not completed till 1946. The slide valves were retained.

As compared with the J6s, their boilers were larger (1,397sq ft of heating surface in the superheated engines against the 1,129sq ft of the J6s), the grate area was the same (19sq ft), the tractive effort was the same, as was also the maximum axle load. The J11 had a Belpaire firebox, whereas the J6 had the normal Doncaster round-top variety.

Like the J6s, the J11s were great favourites with the enginemen and were used on every class of train from pick-up goods to express passenger. In World War I 18 of them were sent to France on loan to the Army.[3]

Of the two types one might have expected the J6 to have been chosen. Far less work would have been needed to modernise them, for they already had piston valves and they had the favoured round-top firebox. However, Thompson chose the J11, perhaps because of its bigger boiler — but he did not need a very strong reason to be swayed against a Gresley design!

In rebuilding, the J11s were provided with long-travel and long-lap piston valves, with the consequent necessary addition of new cylinders. These alterations necessitated pitching the boiler four inches higher, so that a shorter chimney had to be fitted. In addition some fabrication work had to be done on the frames. The original boiler with its Belpaire firebox was retained.

Rebuilding was slow. It went on till 1953, by which time 31 engines had been dealt with. An order for eight more was cancelled in June 1955 under British Railways' Modernisation Plan.[4]

J. F. Harrison says[5] that the rebuilt J11 was a good engine, and certainly better than in its original form. It met the need for a small but powerful 0-6-0 which could be used on the many branch lines where the turnables were too small to take engines of a longer wheelbase.

Unlike the rebuild of the Great Central 2-8-0, there was nothing of the LNER look about the J11 conversion. With its Belpaire firebox and cast-iron chimney of the later Gorton design, its parentage looked obscure and vaguely illegitimate.

The J11s were eventually divided into five 'parts' as under: J11/1 Unrebuilt engines with 3,250 gallon tenders; J11/2 Unrebuilt engines with 4,000 gallon tenders; J11/4 As J11/1 but reduced to LNER loading gauge; J11/5 As J11/2 but reduced to LNER loading gauge; J11/3 Thompson's rebuilt engines.

As in the case of the 0-6-0, Thompson decided that his 2-8-0 for mineral traffic should be a rebuild rather than a new design. He had three classes to choose from: the two-cylinder O1/designed by Gresley for the Great Northern in 1913, the three-cylinder O2 of 1921, also designed by Gresley for the Great Northern, and the Great Central O4 introduced under J. G. Robinson's regime in 1911.

Dimensionally the O1s were very similar to the O4s, but there were only 20 of them because they had been superseded by the three-cylinder O2 class. On the whole they performed well but they were heavy on coal consumption, and were not nearly so successful as the later O2s.[6] Construction of the O2s continued up till 1943, 25 having been turned out after Thompson had become CME. However, even then there were only 66 engines in the class, which was comparatively few compared to the massive number of O4s, and their three cylinders with conjugated valve gear disqualified them for consideration as a standard class.

The O4 had had a very distinguished career. It was chosen by the Ministry of Munitions in World War I as the standard engine for war service, and, as a result, no fewer than 521 of these Great Central engines were eventually built. By the end of that war they had earned a great reputation for sturdiness and for general reliability when maintenance inevitably suffered under the conditions of the time. After the war a large number of engines built for the Army were taken into stock by the Great Central and Great Western Railways; but the width over their cylinders precluded their use over a large proportion of the railways in Great Britain, particularly those which became the LMSR.

In World War II R. A. Riddles, as Deputy Director-General Royal Engineer Equipment at the Ministry of Supply, was responsible for the provision of locomotives to the various theatres of war. The 2-8-0s designed by Stanier had been selected, but it became clear that they could not be built in sufficient quantities within the time required because of the number of man-hours needed in their construction and the shortage of much of the material used in them. Riddles had been tempted at the start of the war to make use of the Great Central 2-8-0s owing to the large numbers available, but he had rejected the idea because over the years they had been modified to suit the particular railways on which they had been working, and they could no longer be considered a standard class. Nevertheless, the needs of the Middle East were so urgent that he did acquire and send to that theatre 91 of these engines, none of which ever came back to the United Kingdom. When difficulties arose over the building of the Stanier engines, he again wondered whether the Robinson 2-8-0s would do instead, but again the lack of standardisation appeared to present insuperable difficulties. The CMEs of the railway companies were well aware of his problem. One day Sir Nigel Gresley called on him and offered to transfer to him almost immediately all the Robinson 2-8-0s in the possession of the LNER if Riddles would undertake to replace them as early as possible with new engines of Gresley's O2 class 2-8-0 design. Riddles says: 'I was profuse in the thanks with which I refused the offer, but I felt that I could build two, or two-and-a-half, of the type I had in mind for every one of the O2 class, apart from the difficulty of finding the materials'.[7] (The engines that Riddles had in mind were, of course, his so-called 'Austerity' 2-8-0s, of which 935 were eventually built. At the end of 1946 190 were purchased by the LNER and added to stock as Class O7.) When Thompson became CME there were 329 O4s running on the LNER.

The first of the Great Central 2-8-0 locomotives was completed at Gorton in September 1911 and it embodied several features of earlier Robinson types. The cylinders, though larger, were the same kind as those of the Atlantics and 4-6-0s of 1903 and the 0-8-0 heavy goods locomotives of 1902. Also common with the 0-8-0s were the 4ft 8in coupled wheels, the axles, and the motion. The boiler, 5ft in diameter and superheated, was the same size as that of the Atlantics. The 21in by 26in cylinders had slide valves, the boiler pressure was 180psi and the grate area was 26.24sq ft. From 1918 to 1921 19 of these 2-8-0s were built with a larger boiler of 5ft 6in diameter; but the first two were rebuilt with the earlier 5ft boiler before the Grouping and the others followed later.

In 1929 Gresley rebuilt two of these engines with an O2 boiler, and subsequently, in 1932-39, another 49 with modified O2 boilers. The first two had to be fitted with longer frames to take the O2 boiler, and hence the decision to provide shortened boilers. The Gorton smokebox was retained. It was not intended to provide all the engines with these boilers, but rather to replace O4 boilers as they wore out and so increase the float of the latter.[8]

Thompson's rebuilding of the O4 was so extensive that it was not really a rebuilding at all but a new engine, because, as stated in Chapter 6, all that was left of the original were the main frames and some wheel centres. The boiler was the B1 type, and this G.C. Gold says, from his experiences at Gorton, cost much less to maintain than the Belpaire boiler which it replaced because of the difficulty of cleaning the firebox crown of the latter.[9] The cylinder and valve gear were identical with the B1. The rebuilt engine was classified O1 and Gresley's first 2-8-0s became O3. Fifty-eight O4s were eventually converted to O1, but conversion then stopped owing to the appearance of the 2-10-0 heavy freight engine which R. A. Riddles produced for British Railways. Of the Thompson O1, J. F. Harrison writes:[10]

'The original GC type O4 was a good locomotive, and worked the GC coal trains well for many years, apart from sterling work in both world wars. The conversion of these engines to take a standard B1 boiler, cylinders and motion helped a little to ease the boiler repair costs. The converted locomotive was never tested against a Gresley three-cylinder 2-8-0, but I doubt if there was much difference between them. Thompson would undoubtedly have converted this engine from three to two cylinders, because three epitomised Gresley, and in any case did not fit in with his ideas on standardisation.'

The rebuild which resulted in the Q1 0-8-0 heavy shunting tank engine was a very much simpler business. Thirteen of the Robinson Q4 0-8-0 freight engines of 1902 were relieved of their tenders, the framing at the back was built up to take a buffer beam and draw gear, and side tanks and bunker were added. This was a ridiculously expensive conversion, however, to provide a quite unnecessary engine.

The most powerful and impressive-looking express passenger engines of the old Great Central were the six four-cylinder 4-6-0s with Stephenson valve gear built from 1917 to 1920. They were: No 6169 *Lord Faringdon*, No 6164 *Earl Beatty*, No 6165 *Valour* (the war memorial engine),11 No 6166 *Earl Haig*, No 6167 *Lloyd George* (this name was removed in August 1923), and No 6168 *Lord Stuart of Wortley*. As mentioned in Chapter 1, they, like their predecessors the two-cylinder 'Sir Sam Fay' class, suffered from their inadequate grate area of 26sq ft and burned prodigious quantities of coal. Gresley, in an effort to improve them, fitted Nos 6166 and 6168 with Caprotti valve gear in 1929. This had some success because the converted engines showed an average saving on coal consumption of 16%, as compared with the piston valve engines. At first there were failures with this gear owing to the cast iron cam operating scrolls breaking, but this was rectified by substituting bronze scrolls. In addition, the working temperature in the cam boxes was at first too high, but this was cured by removing the front end footplating, which

had been raised to form a casing. Two further engines, No 6167 and 6164, were provided with poppet valves in June 1938 and June 1939 respectively, but the Caprotti gear was of a later design with springless steam-operated valves. These two engines were very good indeed, and further experiments would have been undertaken if war had not broken out. That Gresley persisted with these experiments shows the basic soundness of the Gorton designs.[11] The original engines had been classified B3; but after these modifications the class was divided into two parts — the two with the original Stephenson valve gear being B3/1 and the four with Caprotti gear B3/2.

In 1943 the first of the engines to be fitted with Caprotti gear, No 6166, fractured its cylinders, and Thompson seized the opportunity to rebuild it with a B1 boiler, cylinders, and motion. At the same time the nameplate was removed, presumably because it would not fit on the new raised running plate. Though the rebuilt engine was successful, it seems a great pity that this experiment with Caprotti valves was not pursued, rather than curtailed. They were the only Caprotti engines on the LNER, because the Lentz type had been selected for the other locomotives fitted with poppet valves. As regards the two, Spencer says:[12] 'opinions differ as to the comparative advantages of the horizontal Lentz valve and the vertical Caprotti valve; the former is easily accessible, but the latter has the advantage that its weight is not carried by the spindle, and this may have some effect on the even seating of the valve.' The Thompson conversion of the B3 was classified B3/3 and was the only one of the 'Lord Faringdons' to be so rebuilt.

J. F. Harrison says that it was his experience of the Caprotti engines on the Great Central section which led him to welcome the opportunity to fit the much improved English version of the Caprotti gear to No 71000 *Duke of Gloucester* when he was in charge of the building of that engine at Derby. The gear was so good that it enabled this most successful engine to start 500 ton trains on the level with a 30% cut-off and to run with cut-offs as low as 6 and 7%; figures which were not achieved in Harrison's experience by any other locomotive with other types of valve gear.

A very similar conversion to that of No 6166 *Earl Haig* was carried out by Thompson on an engine of the B17 'Sandringham' class; in fact the two conversions were almost identical in appearance and both were really large-wheeled B1s. The first of the B17s to be tackled was No 2871 *Manchester City*, which was renamed *Royal Sovereign* and used on the Royal trains in East Anglia — a typically pompous piece of self-advertisement by Thompson. Nine more B17s were similarly rebuilt. They were, as one would expect, good engines, but certainly no better than the B17s. It is at least questionable as to whether the capital cost of their conversion was justified by the saving in maintenance of the conjugated gear, particularly when balanced against the advantages conferred by three cylinders. Of trials between otherwise similar two-cylinder and three-cylinder 2-6-0 engines of the Southern Railway, the late H. Holcroft wrote:[13] 'The three-cylinder engine was found to be more economical in fuel consumption than the two-cylinder ones with heavy loads. It was freer steaming, smoother riding and could be run with fully opened regulator and a very short cut-off. It was also faster running.'

Thompson's planned conversion of the three-cylinder K3 2-6-0s into two-cylinder engines classified K5 was limited to only one of them, so that it would appear that the exercise was not very successful.

A far more successful venture was the rebuilding of one of Gresley's three-cylinder K4 class 2-6-0s into a two-cylinder engine to provide the prototype for Thompson's standard light mixed traffic engines. Gresley's K4 class of three-cylinder locomotives for the West Highland line had been, as stated in Chapter 5, a brilliant success over this very difficult route. When one of these six engines became due for heavy repairs, Thompson rebuilt it with two cylinders and accepted a drop in tractive effort of about 6,500lb. T. C. B. Miller says that the rebuilt engine was good and less expensive to maintain than the K4, but that it would not have been so satisfactory on the

West Highland line.[14] Standard parts were used in the rebuilding as far as possible, including B1-type cylinders and an O1 type pony truck. The engine as rebuilt did meet a general need and although only one was rebuilt during Thompson's regime, 70 more of the same type, classified K1, were built under Peppercorn with only minor differences from the prototype. The K1 class was intended to replace the J39 and J38 0-6-0s, as well as the K4s. Its maximum axle loading was 19 ton 14cwt and it was graded as RA6.

The only one of Gresley's D49 class that Thompson rebuilt was No 365 *The Morpeth*. This engine had previously had its poppet valve gear modified to make it infinitely variable, instead of having the standard five cut-off positions, and with the valves controlled by steam pressure instead of by springs. However, a lot of trouble was experienced with this modified arrangement; and a year later, in February 1941, the engine had to go into Darlington Works because of damage to the camshaft drive. Because of wartime shortage of materials and labour, No 365 remained for a long time in the Works without having anything done. Thompson then decided to take it as the prototype of a two-cylinder 4-4-0 class, and rebuilt it with inside cylinders of GC 'Director' class pattern, having piston valves operated by Stephenson gear. In its new guise No 365 was tried out for two months during the winter of 1942-43 in comparison with 'Directors' and 'Shires', working from Haymarket shed. It did not perform as well as either of these two classes, and after five years of undistinguished service it was involved in an accident and mercifully disappeared from the scene. An order had been issued for similar rebuilding of four others of the class, but no action was taken and the order was officially cancelled in 1948. Thompson's Class D was therefore limited to one engine.[15] Of it Cecil J. Allen writes: 'This could not have been a very successful effort, as no description of the rebuilt engine ever appeared in the technical press, and it was impossible to obtain any details or photographs from official sources.'[16]

The only Gresley design that Thompson selected for inclusion in his standard classes was the 0-6-0 medium shunting tank engine, originally built for the Great Northern Railway. It had two cylinders and was the best medium shunter the LNER had, so there were no competitors. The first version of 1914 was classified J51 on the LNER. In 1922 a new batch was turned out with slightly larger boilers, which became J50 on the LNER; and all the J51s were gradually rebuilt to conform.

In May 1945 Thompson produced the first of his L1 class two-cylinder 2-6-4 tank engines. Construction continued up till 1950, by which time 100 of these engines had been built. It was intended as a general purpose locomotive for short-haul passenger and goods services, but with a large tank and bunker capacity to enable it to replace tender engines on those workings which had been just beyond the range of existing tank engines. It was intended to replace all other tank engine classes on the LNER, including the V1 and V3 2-6-2s and the N2 and N7 0-6-2s, except those used for shunting. The L1 had 5ft 2in coupled wheels, as compared with the 5ft 8in wheels of the V1, V3, and N2, and the 4ft 10in of the N7. The L1 had the B1 cylinders and motion, but a considerably smaller boiler. The maximum axle load was 20 tons and the route availability 7.

Nobody could claim that the L1s were a success. They were temperamental in their steaming and quite unreliable unless carefully handled by crews who knew them. In addition, they were expensive to maintain; the bearing surfaces in the axleboxes were inadequate for the loads they had to bear and wore out rapidly. This wear, combined with the rapid revolution of the small coupled wheels at speed caused wear in the motion parts and connecting rods.[17]

Thompson carried out one other modification for an entirely different purpose. A locomotive of low RA number being required to haul Directors' and Officers' saloons, Ivatt 4-4-0 No 4075 was selected and embellished suitably for its new and majestic task. It was renumbered 2000, painted green, and given a double-window cab and much polished brass and copper. Only the letters N and E appeared on the tender sides, but between them was emblazoned the magnificent LNER coat of arms, the grant of which had been obtained from the College of Arms soon after the formation of the Company. The heraldic blazon for this was: Argent, on a cross gules, between in the first and fourth quarters a griffin segreant sable, in the second a rose gules leaved and slipped proper, and in the third a thistle also leaved and slipped proper, the Castle of Edinburgh proper between four lions passant guardant gold: crest; on a wreath argent and gules, issuant from clouds of steam proper, the figure of Mercury also proper. In other words, on a white shield was a red cross between, in the first and fourth quarters, a black segreant (ie rampant) griffin, in the second quarter a red rose with stalk and leaves in proper colours, and in the third quarter a thistle in its proper colours. In the middle of the cross was the castle of Edinburgh in its proper colours between, on each limb of the cross, a gold lion of England. Above the shield was Mercury borne on clouds of steam rising from the wreath which always supports a crest. The LNER was the only company to obtain a proper grant of arms. Compared with it the LMS's home-made device was a very poor thing, whilst the GWR had anciently, but illegitimately, purloined the arms of London and Bristol. However, it is British Railways, with its beastly emblem, which must have nearly touched the lowest depths of symbolic art.

It is strange that this magnificent LNER achievement was so seldom used. It appeared on the cab sides of No 4472 *Flying Scotsman* when this engine was given a special finish for the Wembley Exhibition of 1924. But this seems to have been the only locomotive other than No 2000 to bear the arms. When No 2000 was scrapped in 1951 the parts of the tender sides on which the arms had been hand-painted were cut out; one of these is in the possession of J. F. Harrison, whilst G. C. Gold has the other.

Notes

1   The Railway Correspondence & Travel Society, *Locomotives of the LNER* Part 1, pp81-82
2   ibid, Part 5, pp11, 35f
3   ibid, Part 5, pp63f

95

4   Peter Grafton; *Edward Thompson of the LNER*;
    Kestrel Books, 1971, p53
5   J. F. Harrison, letter to the author
6   F. A. S. Brown; *Nigel Gresley: Locomotive Engineer*;
    Ian Allan Ltd, 1961, pp36-37
7   Colonel H. C. B. Rogers; *The Last Steam
    Locomotive Engineer: R. A. Riddles C.B.E.*; George
    Allen & Unwin, 1970, pp106, 108, 115
8   Brown, op cit, p120

9   G. C. Gold, letter to the author
10 J. F. Harrison, letter to the author
11 B. Spencer; 'The Development of LNER Locomotive
    Design 1923-1941' *The Journal of the Institution of
    Locomotive Engineers*, vol XXXXVII (May-June
    1947), pp209-210
12 ibid, p210
13 H. Holcroft; *Locomotive Adventure* vol II; Ian Allan
    Ltd, 1965, p40; and conversation with the author
14 T. C. B. Miller, conversation with the author
15 Grafton, op cit, p84
    RCTS, op cit, Part 4, p93, 97
16 Cecil J. Allen; *The London & North Eastern
    Railway*; Ian Allan Ltd, 1966, pp143-144
17 Grafton, op cit, p80

Below: Class J11/3 0-6-0 No 64417, Thompson's rebuild of a 'Pom-Pom', works hard on Enthorpe bank with a Manchester to Filey express in June 1956. / *J. W. Armstrong*

Top left: J11/3 0-6-0 No 64442 at Mexborough on 17 June 1951.
/ *R. E. Vincent*

Left: Class O1 2-8-0 No 6624, rebuilt from Great Central O4 class.
/ *E. R. Wethersett*

Below: O1 2-8-0 as BR No 63687.
/ *Ian Allan Library*

Above: Class O1 2-8-0 No 63863 climbing up the bank from Staveley on the GCR main line with an up coal train. / *J. S. Hancock*

Right: Class Q1 heavy shunting tank locomotive No 9931, rebuilt from GCR Q4 0-8-0 freight engine. / *E. R. Wethersett*

Far right, top: Q1 0-8-0T No 9936. / *Ian Allan Library*

Far right, below: B3, or 'Lord Faringdon', class 4-6-0 rebuilt as B3/2 with Caprotti valve gear: No 6168 *Lord Stuart of Wortley*. / *Ian Allan Library*

Left: No 6166, originally *Earl Haig*, rebuilt from a B3/2 with four cylinders and Caprotti valve gear to become a B3/3 with two cylinders and a B1 boiler. / *E. R. Wethersett*

Below: B2 class 4-6-0 No 61614 *Castle Hedingham*, photographed in May 1957. / *R. E. Vincent*

Right: B2 No 61671 *Royal Sovereign* in fine shape at Top Shed in 1946. / *E. R. Wethersett*

Centre right: B2 No 61671 *Royal Sovereign* at Marshmoor on an up Cambridge buffet express in 1949. / *E. R. Wethersett*

Bottom right: K5 class 2-6-0 No 206, rebuilt with two cylinders from K3.

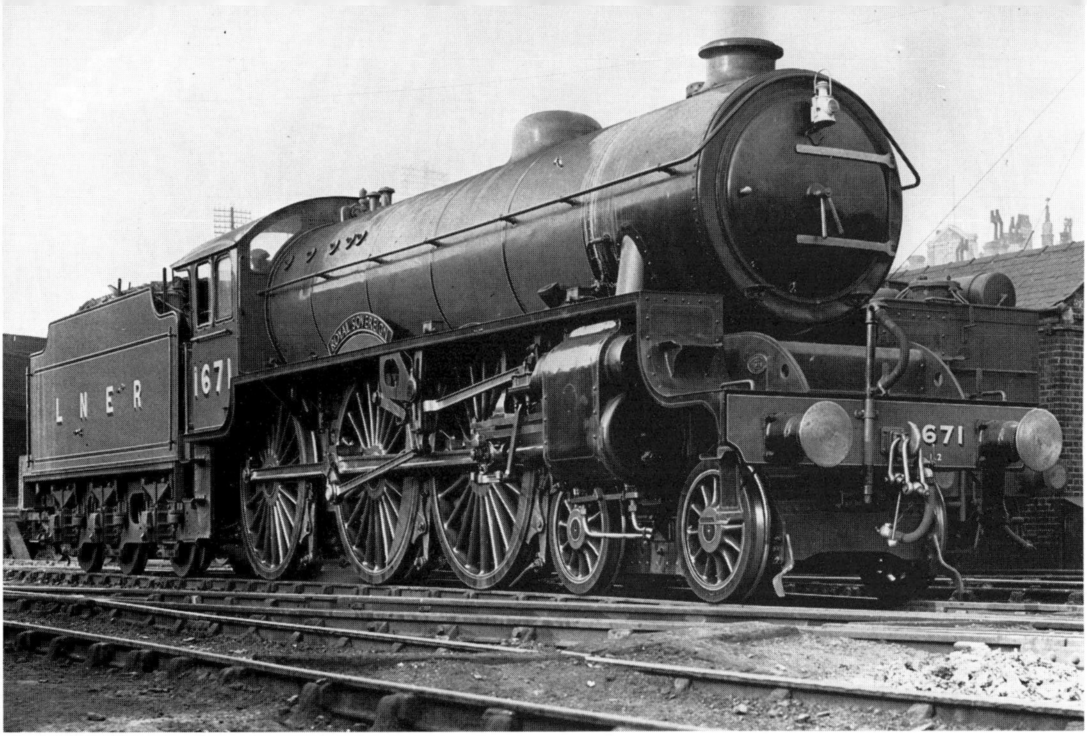
L N E R
1671
671

BRITISH RAILWAYS

206
N E

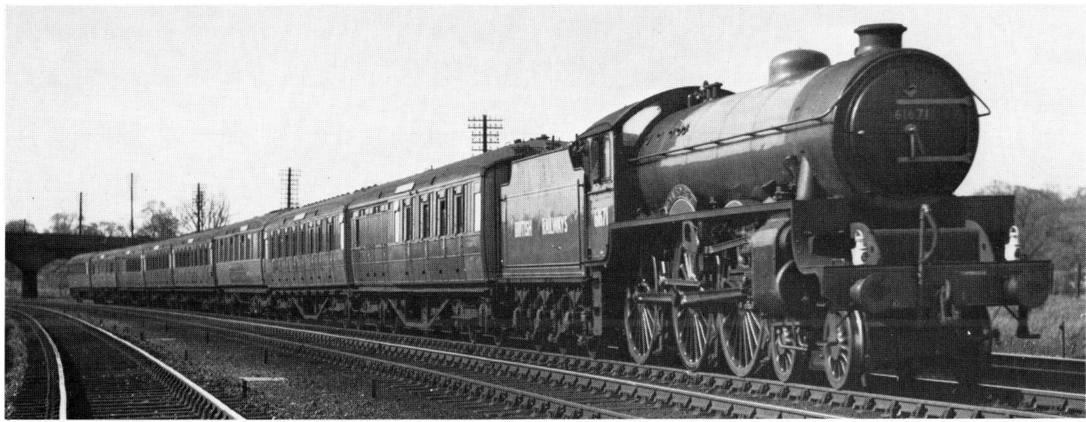

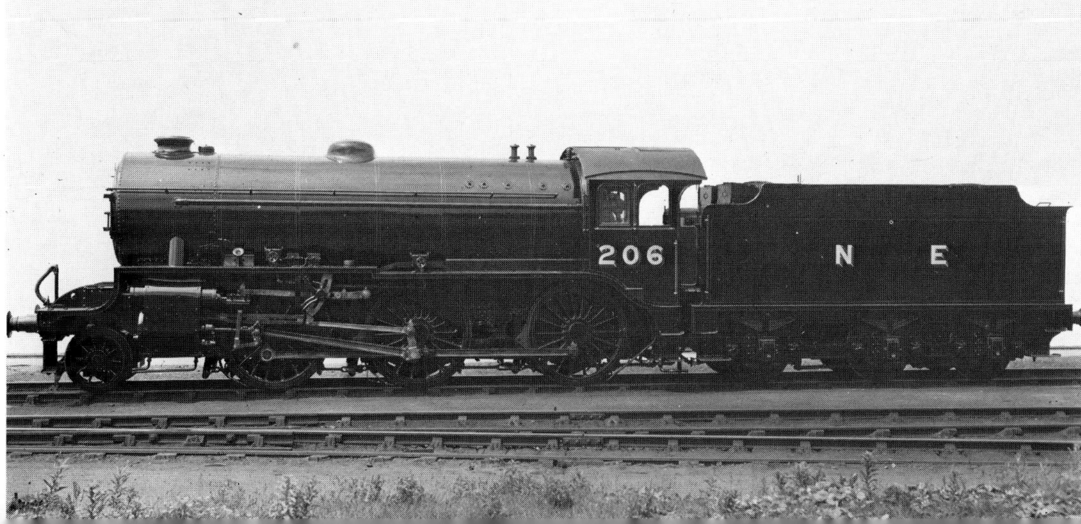

Above left: No 3445 *MacCailin Mor,* rebuilt as a two-cylinder K1 from three-cylinder K4. / *E. R. Wethersett*

Left: K1 class 2-6-0 No 62014 on a Clacton to Liverpool Street train near Colchester on 5 September 1959. / *K. L. Cooper*

Above: K1 2-6-0 No 62036 passing Littlebury on the Cambridge main line on an up goods. / *E. R. Wethersett*

Centre right: The solitary D class 4-4-0 as BR No 62768 *The Morpeth,* rebuilt from the three-cylinder 'Hunt' class locomotive of that name with two inside cyinders. / *H. C. Casserley*

Bottom right: D class *The Morpeth* leaving York on a train for Harrogate. / *K. Field*

215
G N R

L N E R
8905

Left: GNR J50 class 0-6-0T, selected by Thompson as the standard medium shunting engine.

Below left: A J50, No 8905.
/ *E. R. Wethersett*

Right: J50 No 68900 at Beeston on a freight train bound for Ardsley.
/ *Eric Treacy*

Below: L1 class 2-6-4 tank engine No 9000 in green livery on Gateshead shed in July 1946.
/ *E. R. Wethersett*

Above: L1 2-6-4T No 67741 near New Southgate in April
1953. / *E. R. Wethersett*

Below: GNR 4-4-0 No 4075, renumbered 2000 and
embellished to haul directors' saloons, shown at Stratford on
4 August 1945 / *H. C. Casserley*

10. Peppercorn Becomes CME

Arthur Henry Peppercorn, who succeeded Thompson as Chief Mechanical Engineer on 1 July 1946, was a vastly different character to his predecessor. Everybody liked him. 'Arthur was', says his widow (the present Mrs Mather), 'great fun, with a dry sense of humour.' Bad language he heartily disliked. He never swore at his subordinates and told his assistants that if they did so they were 'out'. He was extremely shy in unexpected ways. For instance, he was awarded the OBE in the 1945 Birthday Honours, but he had refused it twice because he was so worried at the idea of going to Buckingham Palace. Eventually the silver-gilt cross of an Officer of the Order was sent to him by post.[1] He was married twice. His first wife was Florence Marjory Faber, whom he married in 1928; but she died only seven years later, in 1935. He met his second wife, Pat, in 1942, when she was Assistant Surveyor with the Coal Commission for the Yorkshire Division. They were married on 14 September 1948.

Peppercorn had always been keen on all forms of sport. In his youth he had played cricket and Rugby football, and in his later days he took up golf and fishing. The latter was his principal hobby, and after his second marriage, he and his wife used to go to Hereford four or five times a year to visit his family and spend some time fishing. He was always a keen family man and kept in close touch with his many sisters and brothers.[2]

The task facing Peppercorn was far from easy. He was very much an admirer of Gresley's work and he was succeeding a CME who had done his utmost to depart from Gresley's features in design, and who had produced locomotives which, as Peppercorn well knew, were, with the exception of the B1, dismal failures.[3] He was not ambitious and viewed with some apprehension the problems he would have to face. Standards of shop repair and shed maintenance were at their lowest ebb and the future, with Nationalisation looming ahead, was uncertain. J. F. Harrison writes:[4] 'He felt the job was a bit too much; but I think only a few of his trusted loyal friends realised this and they certainly never let on. I do not think there is anyone alive today who worked for A.H.P. who does not remember the time with joy and affection.'

The state of maintenance of the existing fleet of locomotives was the greatest worry and to put it right was of far greater importance than the design and construction of new engines. During the war years locomotives had been run for considerably longer periods than was wise between general repairs, owing to the shortage of staff and materials, and many were in a very run-down condition. Furthermore, the repair situation had got worse since the end of the war, so that in early 1947 the LNER Board was receiving complaints from the operating officers that they were having to cancel trains on account of the shortage of locomotives. The workshops could not take any more and engines were standing at sheds awaiting shops for long periods.

J. F. Harrison had established a reputation for getting engines repaired quickly and thoroughly. So, in March 1947, Peppercorn summoned him from Scotland to be Assistant CME, with the specific task of putting the maintenance situation right.

Harrison explains[5] that repairs to locomotives in the main workshops were divided into two categories designated 'Classified' and 'Non-Classified'. The former consisted of 'General', 'Heavy', and 'Light' repairs; whilst the latter referred to 'Casual' repairs, which included accidental damage and odd failures, such as leaking side tanks and loose drag boxes, none of which were considered in the general maintenance scheme.

Of the Classified repairs, General repair was a workshop task and involved the repair of all parts of the locomotive: that is, axleboxes, coupling and connecting rods, cylinders, motion, wheels and axles, boilers and all their fittings, and tenders complete. This repair cancelled mileage and was the basis of the system. Heavy and Light repairs did not cancel mileage. They were unexpected part repairs caused by mishap or failure and were especially specified. To some extent they reflected on the efficiency of the General repair and were therefore expected to be kept to a minimum.

In the early 1920s, when Harrison started his career on the Great Northern Railway, passenger locomotives spent as long as from five to six weeks in the paint shops after repairs, whilst they were given many coats of varnish. At that time, he says, no one seemed to realise that 'time in shops' had to be included in any assessment of the number of locomotives required to run the railway. When he was at Gorton he set about reducing the time in shops. He says:

'This I did successfully, getting down to a maximum of three weeks, and headed the "league table" of the LNER for some years, in spite of having to cope with the heaviest boiler repairs. I looked upon most Light repairs as a disgrace. The governing factor on a time/mileage/hours in steam basis was the boiler (except in Scotland). There were, of course, exceptions. For instance all Pacifics were shopped during the winter months, and in some cases at slightly lower than normal mileage in order to squeeze them into that period. The target that the Regions were set was 4% of locomotives "U&A" shop repairs and 5% "U&A" shed repairs, leaving 91% workable at sheds.'[6]

(Harrison explains that 'U&A' stands for 'under and awaiting', and that it covered those engines agreed for shop repairs but standing at sheds, either unable to move under their own power, or unable to be accepted by shops.)

The problem facing Harrison in 1947 was so vast that, he says, 'It was necessary to pluck from the skies another workshops, for the LNER Works had no spare capacity. So we approached Vickers Armstrong, at their Scotswood Works in Newcastle, who had suitable workshops for the complete repair of locomotives, including the boilers. They gave us invaluable help until we had dealt with the backlog of repairs.'

With regard to boiler repairs in general, Harrison says that it is interesting that on the Great Central section boilers required new fireboxes every three or four years, whilst on the Great Northern and Great Eastern sections the periods were from 10 to 12 years and in Scotland from about 35 to 50 years. The reason was the difference in the water. The Great Central had the exceptionally hard water of Derbyshire and Nottinghamshire. The Great Northern and Great Eastern, on the other hand, had the type of water and the length of time between boiler repairs which were about average for the whole of England. Scotland was, of course, exceptionally fortunate in the water available for locomotives. Harrison adds that conditions in Scotland led to almost paradoxical failures. Because fireboxes lasted so long, a normal repair period of say three years was a small percentage of the firebox life cycle. Very often, therefore, after the thirtieth year of the firebox life, the boiler shop foreman had difficulty in deciding whether the fracture in the root of tubeplate radii or the condition by 'sound' of a firebox stay was good enough to last another period of service, ie three years. Many times they judged matters correctly, but it was bad policy to have a failure, with consequent early shopping, during the locomotive shed life, and this did happen too frequently, particularly with boiler side stays. There were more broken stays per week at sheds in Scotland than on the whole of the rest of the LNER. When Harrison went to Scotland he found this situation accepted; but he had it promptly altered by ensuring that specified areas of stays were removed at, say, the twentieth year, and by tightening up the maximum time which could be allowed for firebox plate fractures to develop. This increased the cost of workshop repairs, but it reduced the expensive shed repairs, and it also increased the availability of locomotives. The result was a reduction in the Company's overall costs.

In the past, Harrison says, and up to the time of Nationalisation there had always been rivalry between the Chief Mechanical Engineer and the Locomotive Running Department, except when the latter came under the CME. Each department blamed the other for efficiency failures in locomotive performance. On the other hand when the Board of a company put the LRD under the CME, all locomotive deficiencies were of course the responsibility of the latter; with the consequence that he took care that if defects existed in either workshops or sheds they were soon rectified. Harrison adds: 'The reason this did not happen often was the reluctance of the Operating Officer or Divisional General Manager to concede so much power to the CME. At the root of this reluctance frequently lay the administrative officer's jealousy of the professional engineer; and if the engineer was a bit "bloody-minded" considerable friction resulted.'

Because Harrison's time was so much taken up at Doncaster with the repair situation, he did not have a lot to do with design during the early months of his new appointment. As stated in Chapter 6, B. Spencer, who had been Gresley's Assistant (Technical), had been posted away from Doncaster by Thompson when he became CME, and replaced by D. R. Edge. Spencer was a most able engineer and Thompson's dismissal of him was, as Harrison says, sheer vindictiveness. When Peppercorn took over he reinstated Spencer, but in the meantime E. Windle, the Chief Draughtsman, had in practice assumed the position which had been occupied by Spencer. The result was, as Harrison writes:[7] 'Windle, Spencer, and myself all discussed what was required and what should be done. We all (including A.H.P.) had the same object, namely to produce a more reliable Gresley locomotive; and we wished to eliminate from the basic Gresley design concept those things which had proved unsatisfactory, or which changed maintenance practices had made more difficult. A.H.P. took our views and digested them before passing them to Windle to turn into practical designs.'

At this stage it is worth reviewing the vexed question as to whether the expensive Belpaire boiler designed by G. J. Churchward for the Great Western Railway, and subsequently adopted by the London Midland & Scottish and British Railways, was a better choice than the cheaper boiler with round-top firebox favoured by Doncaster and the London & North Eastern Railway.

The highly efficient Belpaire boiler with coned barrel and curved side plates of the firebox had been developed by Churchward into its final form in September 1902. It was first fitted in that month to the 'Atbara' class 4-4-0 engine *Mauritius*, the prototype of the famous 'Cities'. It is a mark of Churchward's genius that no better boiler was ever designed, and that it was adopted, virtually unaltered, for the last steam locomotives designed in Great Britain about half a century later.

But Churchward's boiler was expensive — far more expensive than the round-top parallel (except on the biggest engines) boiler preferred by successive Chief Mechanical Engineers at Doncaster. It is of some importance, therefore, to consider why Churchward chose it.

Until the end of the nineteenth century the normal firebox used in Great Britain was of the type then known as 'Crampton' (as it is still so known in France), in which the outer firebox was formed by a prolongation of the boiler barrel, and was thus round-topped, whilst the inner firebox had a flat or slightly curved top. A variation of this was a boiler with the round-top outer firebox raised above the barrel of the boiler to get more steam space. All Archibald Sturrock's engines for the Great Northern had this feature, which he had probably copied from Daniel Gooch's later engines for the Great Western, because Sturrock had been Works Manager at Swindon before going to the Great Northern.

In 1866 W. Bouch had designed a firebox with a flat top to the outer casing which was fitted to his 'long boiler' goods engines for the

Stockton & Darlington Railway from 1866 to 1874; but it differed from the later Belpaire firebox in that the top of the outer firebox was lower than the top of the boiler barrel.[8] The Belpaire firebox was so named after its designer, who fitted it to engines of the Belgian State Railways. The first Belpaire fireboxes constructed in Great Britain were made by Beyer Peacock & Co in 1872 for the Belgian Malines-Ternenzen Railway.[9] Beyer Peacock subsequently built locomotives with Belpaire fireboxes for the Belgian State Railways. Next door to the Beyer Peacock Works were those of the Manchester Sheffield & Lincolnshire Railway, whose Chief Draughtsman had previously been with Beyer Peacock. He recommended that the MSLR should adopt the Belpaire firebox. His claims as to its superiority could be easily assessed because Beyer Peacock's engines were handy for all MSL men at Gorton to see. The Chief Draughtsman's advice was taken and in 1891 Thomas Parker's 9C class of 0-6-2 tanks were turned out from Gorton with Belpaire fireboxes, the first engines on any British railway to have them.[10] Thereafter the Belpaire firebox was adopted as standard on MSL and, later, Great Central engines.

Churchward was attracted by the ease of direct staying with Belpaire fireboxes and with the increased steam space and water surface. These features are obvious in the study of the cross section of a Belpaire firebox as compared with one of the Crampton type.

In his famous paper 'Large Locomotive Boilers', read to the Institute of Locomotive Engineers in February 1906, Churchward said:

'The gradual extension of the practice of making the top of the firebox and casing flat, instead of round, is noticeable. On the Great Western Railway less trouble has been experienced with the flat-top firebox than with the round top, although no sling stays of any kind are used. The flat top has the important advantage of increasing the area of the water-line at the hottest part of the boiler, and so materially contributes to the reduction of foaming. This, combined with the coned connection to the barrel, has enabled the dome, always a source of weakness, to be entirely dispensed with and drier steam obtained. The author some years ago made an experiment to settle this much disputed point. Two identical engines and boilers were taken, one boiler having a dome in the usual position on the barrel, the other having no dome, the steam being taken by a pipe from the top of the flat firebox casing. The engine without the dome proved to be decidedly freer from priming than the other. The liberal dimension of 2ft between the top of the firebox and the inside of the casing no doubt contributed to this satisfactory result. The coned barrel connection, in addition to providing a greater area of water line, also gives a larger steam capacity, and by the larger diameter being arranged to coincide with the line of the firebox tube-plate, much more water space at the sides of tubes is possible. On consideration of the great intensity of temperature at the firebox plate, as compared with that at the smokebox plate, the advantage of the arrangement is obvious.'

In connection with the above, A. Chapelon points out, in a letter to the author, that when Patrick Stirling fitted domeless boilers to his Great Northern engines, he avoided the risk of priming by lowering the top of the inner firebox. This reduced the circulation of the water in the boiler; but such a reduction was not acceptable in Great Western engines because they had to work so much harder. Churchward, to avoid reducing the circulation, increased the distance between the tops of the inner and outer fireboxes by raising the latter.

There were troubles, however, with the first Churchward Belpaire boilers. Churchward's first 4-6-0 locomotive, No 100, suffered from broken stays and cracks at the junction of the boiler barrel and firebox. Investigation showed that the boiler circulation was indifferent and, as a result, Churchward increased the size of the water legs of the firebox by curving the side plates. The resulting sweep of the firebox ensured the success of the Churchward standard boiler.[11]

However, it is conceivable that these troubles were more prone to arise with a straight-sided Belpaire firebox than with the round-top type, because there does not appear to be any record of similar troubles with the Doncaster round-top firebox with either coned or parallel boiler barrel. On the other hand, the 'Royal Scots' of the LMS, with their straight-sided Belpaire fireboxes had a poor mileage between boiler repairs. When Stanier rebuilt them with a coned barrel and the shape of the Swindon firebox the mileage was nearly doubled.[12]

J. F. Harrison, in a letter to the author, outlines the case for the round top firebox as follows:

'A Belpaire firebox may have been theoretically cheaper to maintain than a round-top one, but I have no evidence to this effect. In fact, in my experience the reverse was the case, and when one considers the argument two points seem to me to be relevant:

1 Under pressure circular section vessels or spheres are acknowledged to be the most satisfactory, and are certainly the cheapest to manufacture.
2 It could be said that the final development of the Belpaire, as it appeared on the LMS Pacifics, brought out the need for very full radii at all original design sections; that is, a return towards the principle outlined in 1 above.'

The 'Austerity' 2-8-0 and 2-10-0 locomotives designed by R. A. Riddles had parallel boilers and round-top fireboxes. He introduced this type of boiler for ease of manufacture and economy in materials, rather than the more expensive LMS type of tapered Belpaire boiler. The round-top boiler compared satisfactorily with the LMS type of the Stanier 2-8-0s, both in steaming capacity and economy of maintenance, particularly as regards the 2-10-0. This is shown in a letter written by Major-General D. J. McMullen, Director of Transportation, to Riddles on 15 February 1945, saying that he had just come back from a visit to the British Liberation Army and had to let him know how excellently the 'Austerity' 2-8-0s and 2-10-0s were doing. He continues: 'Everyone

loves the 2-10-0. It is quite the best freight engine ever turned out in Great Britain and does well on even Belgian "duff", which is more like porridge than coal. The 2-8-0s have trouble for steaming on this muck alone, but if they can get 25% of Dutch lump coal mixed with it they do all right.' On 4 January he wrote to Riddles again, saying: 'I have yet to see in Europe anything to touch your 2-10-0 weight for weight.'

Later, when he was Member for Mechanical and Electrical Engineering on the Railway Executive, Riddles noted that there seemed little to choose between the B1 4-6-0 of the LNE, with its round-top firebox and parallel boiler, and the Class 5 4-6-0 of the LMS. The decision to fit the Churchward type of Belpaire firebox to his Standard engines for British Railways was due to its proven excellence and the highly developed technique adopted at Crewe, in the production of Belpaire boilers, where all the Standard boilers were built; but Riddles believes that there was, in fact, no more than a marginal difference between it and the cheaper Doncaster round-top variety.[13]

Harrison points out[14] that the boiler accounts for the largest item in repair costs. The LMS carried out some very expensive water softening, with the result that their mileage between General repairs was increased as compared with the LNE; but the water softening was not included in their repair costs. When it ultimately was included and real comparative costs got out, the LNE figures were as good as, if not better than, any of the other Companies.

Gresley had been very impressed with the very successful coned boiler with wide Belpaire firebox of the Pennsylvania Railroad K4 Pacifics, and he copied it in general when he built his Pacifics in 1922, but his firebox, though wide, had a round-top instead of the K4 Belpaire.

On the evidence examined, one might perhaps conclude that there was little or no difference between a well designed round-top boiler and the Churchward type of Belpaire boiler, both in steaming capacity and in maintenance costs, though the latter was more expensive to construct. On the other hand, the straight-sided Belpaire firebox seems to have been both more expensive to build and also to maintain that the round-top variety. However, there is a lot more to boiler design than the shape of the firebox. Churchward's boilers were beautifully designed, but so also were those of Ivatt and Gresley.

Notes
1 Mrs Mather, conversation with the author
2 W. H. Mather, letter to the author
3 J. F. Harrison, letter to the author
4 ibid
5 ibid
6 ibid
7 ibid
8 E. L. Ahrons: *The British Steam Railway Locomotive 1825-1925*; The Locomotive Publishing Co, 1927, p173
9 ibid, p237
10 ibid, p310
   George Dow; *Great Central*, vol II; Locomotive Publishing Co, 1962, p261
11 K. J. Cook; 'The Late G. J. Churchward's Locomotive Development on the Great Western Railway'; *Journal of the Institution of Locomotive Engineers*, Paper No 492 (March-April 1950)
12 Sir William Stanier; 'George Jackson Churchward, Chief Mechanical Engineer, Great Western Railway'; *Transactions of the Newcomen Society* XXX (1960)
13 R. A. Riddles, conversation with the author
14 J. F. Harrison, letter to the author

Below: A Riddles 'Austerity' 2-8-0 in LNER livery. / G. O. P. Pearce

Right: Peppercorn and, indeed, Thompson inherited a fleet of locomotives badly neglected in the war: even the A4s were not immune, epitomised by No 4498 *Sir Nigel Gresley* bringing empty stock past Shepreth on 4 September 1943. The chime whistle is still on though! / E. R. Wethersett

Below right: The B1s greatly assisted the hard-pressed locomotive running departments, particularly in East Anglia. No 8307 *Blackbuck* waits at Ely with the Colchester to York train in July 1945; O. S. Nock on the footplate. / E. R. Wethersett

Right: Even so, locomotives and trains were smartly kept in the early postwar period, such as A3 No 60059 *Tracery* at the head of the down 'Queen of Scots' at Lofthouse in August 1948. / *E. R. Wethersett*

Below: Riddles 2-8-0 No 63118 on an up freight train at Cadwell near Hitchin on 28 May 1949. / *R. E. Vincent*

11. The Peppercorn Pacifics

When Thompson retired it is likely that he expected that the whole 43 of his 6ft 2in Pacifics of the A2/3 class and the 39 6ft 8in Pacifics of the A1/1 class (similar to his rebuilding of the *Great Northern*), which had been authorised, would be built. He little knew that his drawing officer staff, even before his retirement, had been thinking about these new engines and had determined to try and prevent them being built with the outside cylinders so far back, and to influence a return to the more orthodox arrangement. B. C. Symes writes: 'The general layout of the first "Peppercorn" Pacific was in fact on my drawing board (except for the front end) before Pepp took over.'[1]

When Peppercorn assumed office, he reinstated B. Spencer in his old post. However, D. R. Edge, whom Thompson had installed in replacement of Spencer, had not been given the same functions, and in practice it was E. Windle, the Chief Draughtsman, who replaced Spencer in matters relating to locomotive design. As a result, under the Peppercorn regime, Harrison, Spencer, and Windle discussed amongst themselves locomotive design policy, and submitted their agreed views to Peppercorn. The CME then considered them, made his decisions, and instructed Windle to turn them into practical designs. Agreement was not difficult as all had the same object, which was to produce a more reliable Gresley-type locomotive; that is to say, a locomotive without those Gresley features which had

proved unsatisfactory or which changed practices and conditions had made more difficult to maintain. Harrison says that Gresley did not bother a great deal about the cost of maintenance. Harrison, however, had had to spend a lot of his time in repairing bad features in the locomotives of constituent companies, and even in some of Gresley's own design. The others agreed with him that it was important to incorporate in the design everything that would reduce maintenance costs to a minimum; such as, roller bearing axleboxes, cast steel wherever possible, and minor design details to prevent cylinders, hornblocks, stays, etc, working loose. Conjugated valve gear was so expensive in maintenance by a largely inexperienced staff that it would be much better to design a separate valve gear for the middle cylinder. Thought was indeed given to the possibility of designing much larger bearings for the conjugated gear's two-to-one beam, but the matter was not pursued.[2]

Apart from technical problems, the morale of the staff was none too good after Thompson's retirement. Harrison mentions:[3] 'The difficulties in getting the best out of the staff, who felt that their previous boss had been so against everything they believed in, that they could not enthuse over anything that smacked of Thompson.' There was therefore a psychological need to return to more traditional Doncaster practice — a need which made itself felt down the locomotive chain from the drawing office to the footplate. Peppercorn certainly did not contemplate any radical departures from Gresley's locomotive standards. Oliver Bulleid is said to have remarked to him on one occasion, 'Pepp, if you design an express locomotive with five driving wheels, your name is made.' Whether exaggerated or not, this remark does typify Bulleid's outlook on locomotive matters, which horrified Peppercorn.[4]

The first decision made by Peppercorn as regards the construction of Pacifics was that the Thompson A2 locomotives (soon to be redesignated A2/3) would be limited to 15 and that the remainder of the 6ft 2in engines that had been authorised should be built to the new design which he had approved. Windle, as we have seen, had already anticipated the principal features of the new Pacific and the drawing office produced the first outline drawing in August 1946. The most obvious difference from the Thompson engines was that the bogie was back in the conventional position with the outside cylinders between its wheels and the long external exhaust ducts had consequently disappeared. As a result of later discussion the banjo dome and perforated steam collector were reintroduced. A more controversial decision was to have a self-cleaning smokebox, and as the smokebox was shorter than that of the A2/3 there was not room for the double blastpipe and Kylchap exhaust. The engine therefore had a single chimney; but to many who had been appalled by Thompson's horrible transformation of the *Great Northern*, this new Pacific with its passable resemblance to an A3 may have brought assurance of the return of the classic era. The order placed with Darlington for 13 A2/3 Pacifics was cancelled, and replaced by an order on Doncaster for 20 A2s; so that there would be 15 A2/3s and 35 A2s — an increase of seven on Thompson's original order. However, the last 20 of the A2s were cancelled by British Railways on 4 May 1948 on account of the new locomotive design policy; so that only 15 were actually built. These 15 were numbered 525-539, becoming in due course Nos 60525-60539 of British Railways.

The single chimney with self-cleaning smokebox did not help the steaming and on 6 May 1948 Doncaster Works were instructed to fit a Kylchap double blastpipe and chimney to the last A2 of the order, No 60539, as well as to the new A1 class Pacifics, of which the first was approaching completion. The length of the smokebox was not altered so there was no room for the self-cleaning apparatus.

There is a rather amusing story in connection with the building of No 60539. Peppercorn was walking round Doncaster Works and saw the engine being fitted with a double chimney. He asked why and was told it was on Harrison's orders. Peppercorn promptly tackled Harrison and said he thought that he was the CME. Harrison replied that Peppercorn had told him to arrange for the double chimney. 'Oh, did I?', said Peppercorn![5]

The steaming of No 60539 left nothing to be desired, so in 1949 five more of the A2s were given the double Kylchap arrangement: Nos 60526, 60529, 60532, 60533, and 60538.

Steaming troubles with single chimney engines having self-cleaning smokeboxes was not confined to the A2s. The V2 2-6-2s which had been fitted with similar smokeboxes also suffered. In March 1950, when there were 11 single-chimney A2s in Scotland, it was concluded there that the self-cleaning apparatus, rather than the chimney, was to blame, and in due course Scottish Region submitted a report to Doncaster. However, as the B1 4-6-0s had self-cleaning smokeboxes which gave every satisfaction, it was decided to try modifying the A2 smokebox on the lines of the B1, which had a shorter blastpipe and a longer chimney. Authority was given to alter five of the A2s — Nos 60525, 60530, 60531, 60535, and 60537. This improved the steaming of all these engines, though there was some increase in coal consumption.[6]

Of the above-mentioned V2s, one of them was sent to the Swindon Test Plant for investigation into ways of improving the steaming. There the self-cleaning plates were removed and modifications were made to the proportions of the chimney liner, cowl, and blastpipe top. It was reported that the evaporation rate was more than doubled. However, there must be a suspicion that this was a particularly bad engine, because P. N. Townend's opinion of this modification has been reported in Chapter 5. This opinion is supported by similar modifications which were made as a result of the Swindon report to No 60525 in December 1953 and No 60530 in February 1954. Ferryhill reported that No 60525 showed no improvement; in fact, on the contrary, tests made when the engine was engaged on the heaviest duties showed that the steaming was somewhat impaired and the coal consumption was high. In November the engine was 'shopped' at Doncaster, when the steaming was improved, though still greatly inferior to that of the double chimney engines. By this time four more single-chimney A2s (60527, 60528, 60534, and 60536) had been subjected to the Swindon modification, but with the blast pipe tops slightly reduced in diameter. Somewhat lengthy experiments were terminated on 30 January 1957 with the comment that there was little to choose between any of these arrangements, but that the single chimney A2s would be modified to the B1 class proportions that Nos 60531, 60535, and 60537 still had. By this time all the A1s, as well as the five A2s so fitted, had been steaming perfectly for eight years with the Kylchap double blastpipe and chimney. It seems extraordinary, therefore, that the single chimney A2s were not converted to that arrangement. It would appear, however, from Townend's experience recorded in Chapter 5, that about this period there was a decided preference at Doncaster for the Swindon exhaust proportions rather than the double Kylchap.

In addition to 16 A1 Pacifics authorised under the 1945 programme, Thompson obtained on 2 May 1946 authority for a further 33 on the 1946 programme, making a total (including the A1/1 *Great Northern*), of 40 engines. In August 1948 Peppercorn obtained authority for 10 more on the 1949 programme. But except for the *Great Northern*, all these engines were of Peppercorn and not Thompson design. The drawing office had started work on them before Thompson's retirement, but they had started at the back end (which was all right) and had made just sufficient progress to keep Thompson satisfied.[7]

The A1 design which was finally adopted was basically the same as the A2, with the same arrangement of cylinders and inside valve gear and the same boiler. The coupled wheel base was longer on account of the larger coupled wheel diameter, and the smokebox was consequently made 1ft 9in longer than that of the A2. Originally it was proposed to have a single chimney and self-cleaning smokebox, but the latter idea was discarded and the double Kylchap exhaust and chimney were adopted as stated above. To the casual eye the only difference in appearance from the A2 class lay in the small splashers over the big driving wheels. Five of the A1s in the last batch built at Doncaster (Nos 60153-7) had Timken roller bearings on all axles with the object of increasing the mileage between general repairs.

The first of the A1 class was turned out from Doncaster in August 1948 and all 49 were in service before the end of 1949. As the railways had been nationalised before any of the engines had been completed they never bore the initials LNER on their tenders, but 36 of them were originally painted in LNER green.[8]

The principal dimensions of the two classes are given below, those common to both being in the middle:

	A2		A1
Cylinders (3)		19in × 26in	
Heating Surface, sq ft			
Firebox		245.3	
Tubes		1,211.57	
Flues		1,004.5	
Superheater		679.67	
Total		3,141.04	
Grate area, sq ft		50	
Boiler pressure, psi		250	
Coupled wheels	6ft 2in		6ft 8in
Tractive effort, lb	40,430		37,347
Weight, engine	101 ton		104 ton 2cwt
Adhesive weight		66 ton	
Max axle load		22 ton	
Engine wheel base	34ft 4in		36ft 3in

The inside connecting rod of both classes was 7ft 2in between centres, as on the A2/3s, but the outside connecting rods were 10ft in length. All three cylinders were inclined at 1 in 30. Of these alterations B. C. Symes comments that the longer outside connecting rod resulted in more even valve events and less pressure on the slide bars, and that the better use of the steam pipes in the smokebox allowed more flexibility in the pipes and reduced the strain on the joints.[9]

During April and May 1949 trials were held between A2 No 60538 *Bronzino* and A1 No 60114 *W. P. Allen* to compare their performance and coal consumption. Both engines had double chimneys and were, in fact, nearly identical except for the difference in size of the driving wheels. The trials consisted in hauling trains of nearly 500 tons on schedules demanding medium power and trains specially made up to 600 tons requiring a high power output. Both engines performed well and the riding was assessed as good, though the A2 had a tendency to nose and roll more than the A1 when entering curves, and it was assumed that this was due to the difference in wheel diameter. The coal consumption of the A2 was rather more than the A1 on the medium power trials, but less on the high power trials (44.5lb per mile, as compared with 47.5). Both engines burnt more than the A4 did during the 1949 interchange trials; but the validity of this comparison was doubtful because the conditions were different and the A4 was given coal of a higher calorific value. As the 500 ton trains did not require an output of high power, except for small portions of each trip, the results did not reflect the full capacity of the big grate, which was considerably larger in area than that of the A4.

It was soon found that the Peppercorn Pacifics were not as smooth riding as the A4s and were liable to give sudden lurches at the cab end. R. C. Bond rode on an A1 and says that it hunted badly.[10] J. F. Harrison says, 'The Peppercorn A2s, when first built, were liable to lurch in an alarming manner at speeds in excess of 90mph.'[11] However, there was considerable variation between individual engines. P. N. Townend writes:[12]

'The A3, A4, and V2 rode well in my experience; some A1s rode equally as well and others did not. It is fair to say that they were more sensitive to track conditions. For example, there used to be a crossing at the south end of New Southgate Station where the A1 would usually give a lurch and immediately settle down again. The lurch was probably more noticeable on the A1 because your head was in line with the heavy brass casting which was the top runner of the cab sliding window, and if not prepared you could get a nasty crack on the head. The seats were lower on the Gresley locomotives and this did not happen.'

T. C. B. Miller, writing of the A1s, says:[13]

'The drivers complained bitterly about rough riding, particularly the Kings Cross men I seem to remember. I certainly recall two trips I made; the first to see for myself what one was like, and I certainly got some hefty thumps in the ribs from the cill of the cab window as I sat in the fireman's seat. There was a characteristic sideways lurch at the rear end when running at speed. In September 1957 I made another run, this time on 60153, one of the roller bearing engines, and I had my father with me who was just over 80. I was a bit apprehensive because at that age one can easily be frightened. I remember he was not frightened but he did not enjoy it much. Of course there are many records of fine performances by A1s, and many at over 100mph, so they must have been put right eventually.'

There was obviously something not quite right which was affecting the riding of the engines; but what? P. N. Townend discusses the problem at some length as follows:[14]

'Some of the A1s at Kings Cross gave rise to complaints of bad riding. At that time we had 12 allocated along with 19 A4s and 11 A3s. The worst individual locomotive at that time was 60157, fitted with roller bearings. The engine oscillated from side to side on straight track as soon as you reached 60mph, and did not stop the continuous side to side movement until you hit a curve. The oscillation would then stop dead as though someone had switched it off; but it would start again as soon as you got on straight track. The locomotive 'crabbed' its way along straight track, with a lateral movement of the engine/tender fall plate of about 12 inches. This was the only locomotive I had like this, and it was decided, after examining it thoroughly, to try and send it to the Works. The Chief Mechanical & Electrical Engineer would not accept it, at first, under the normal shopping procedure, because it was not due for Work repair; but after some weeks I managed to persuade one of his technical staff to go back on the locomotive, following a visit by him to Kings Cross. It was put on the 4.50pm Pullman, first stop York, and the driver advised appropriately. By Hitchin the Technical Assistant had accepted the point as proven and requested the driver to ease off, as he was not sure otherwise that they were going to get there.

'The locomotive, 60157, was sent to Works the next day and stripped down. The Chief Mechanical & Electrical Engineer personally examined the components laid out on the side of the pit, and in due course it was announced that there was nothing wrong with the locomotive, which was reassembled and returned to Kings Cross a few days later. It rode well on its return and went on to run 197,000 miles before going to Works for a Classified Repair — the highest mileage we ever got out of any locomotive. I made enquiries at the time about the bogie side control springs on 60157, asking if they had been renewed at the examination in Works; but I was told that all the springs had been put into a bosh to be cleaned, along with those off other locomotives, and that no one knew which springs were refitted on 60157.

'Many of the A1s at Kings Cross were regularly manned for a time, but gradually most of the crews requested A4s, mainly because the A1s had this tendency to lurch at the cab end. Driver Hoole asked if he could change his A1 for an A4 as his mate had difficulty sometimes in getting the coal into the firehole door; but he emphasised that he had nothing against the locomotive himself, because otherwise it was excellent and did not worry him. He did not, though, want his mate to transfer. Driver Arthur Davis had 60149 for many months and asked if I could stop his engine riding across the fields. He was not sure at times that it was on the rails at all.

'All the depot could generally do with such complaints was to tighten up the drawgear between engine and tender. If this was screwed as tight as possible with the intermediate buffers, this did help to steady the locomotive. The Cartazzi and tender bearings were checked for end float, and these were also renewed if necessary.

'On the other hand 60156, a roller bearing locomotive like 60157, was regularly manned the whole time it was allocated to Kings Cross and was never the subject of any complaints.

It was probably the best locomotive we ever had, as it ran 96,000 miles in approximately 12 months, which was considerably more than the A4s ever attained.

'Having got nowhere with 60157 in discovering the basic cause of the intermittently unsatisfactory riding of certain locomotives, No 60136, the next locomotive out of Works, was chosen for further checks. The reason for the choice was that as it was just out of a Works repair the CM&EE could hardly blame depot maintenance for its condition. It was no worse or better than most of the other locomotives and it did exhibit the tendency to lurch occasionally at the back end which I always felt could be dangerous. As we believed the trouble stemmed from the bogie, I asked for the locomotive to be tested with an A4 bogie fitted. This could not be done as a straight exchange due to the design of the locomotive, but an A4 type bogie was made up at Doncaster and fitted for a time. The locomotive was tested first with the indicator shelters on and it was found that the power produced at each stroke of the middle cylinder varied considerably. This was eventually put down to the expansion of the main frames when the engine got hot, so the usual expansion allowance for the middle valve spindle was discontinued. However, this was not, and could not be, the cause of the trouble, which in my view was due to the tension of two tons on the bogie side control springs being insufficient. I have seen or heard somewhere that J. F. Harrison had said that there was some divergence of opinion as to the load to put on these springs, and I think he favoured four tons, but I cannot find this anywhere now.

'60136 was at this time, unfortunately, transferred to Doncaster — and Doncaster never complained about the riding of the A1s. However, my own Inspector checked 60136 one day for me and said that the riding was now satisfactory with the altered bogie. Whether the bogie side control springs were ever changed or more tension put on them is not known. It could well have been done without depots being aware of it but there were no further investigations after that on 60136 and the subject died.

'It is perhaps worth mentioning that the Cartazzi slopes on the A1s were found to have been incorrectly designed, when the subject was investigated in the late 1950s. The same Cartazzi drawing had been marked up for all the 50sq ft grate locomotives as had been used for all those with the 41.25sq ft grates, although the distance from the trailing wheels of the former was greater, and the angles of the slopes or taper blocks should have been altered as well as the radius struck from the trailing coupled wheels. One A1 was altered to the recalculated dimensions, but no one could observe any difference. In any case this difference was so small that it was not worth bothering about.

'I tested 60156 one day from Grantham to Kings Cross, with the regular crew instructed to go as hard as they could down the bank at Stoke, and it never budged. The A1s, despite this tendency to lurch, did run more miles than any of the other Pacifics at Kings Cross, and generally were good reliable locomotives with much better availability than the Gresley varieties.'

Townend, at the time of these events, was Assistant District Motive Power Superintendent, Kings Cross.

J. F. Harrison has some interesting comments on Townend's letter. He had been transferred to Derby some years before Townend was conducting his investigations. He shows, however, that he was well aware of the trouble and its cause before his departure. Presumably, as a matter of policy, it was decided that it would be inadvisable to make the weakness of the bogies generally known for fear of undermining confidence, because it would take a long time to alter the large number of Peppercorn and Thompson Pacifics and the weakness was not considered dangerous. Harrison writes:[15]

'The lightly loaded side control springs and fairly light main bearing springs caused trouble which was not solved until after the Peppercorn A2s had been reported to us as bad riders at high speed. I came into the picture at this time, and we started afresh to design, or rather alter, the spring features to

get this bogie to behave as well as Gresley's had. It took time, feeling our way gradually towards the right solution. This was eventually found, as was demonstrated by the riding of 60156, and also 60157 when the side control springs were changed — for this is obviously what happened when the engine was sent on that special visit to the Works.

'In the process of arriving at the right answer, whilst I do not remember having said that four tons loading on the side control springs was right, I can well believe that I did; because when one is trying to persuade a reluctant designer to alter something, it is as well to go too far to start with! Actually I believe a satisfactory figure was achieved at 3.2 tons.'

It seems clear, then, that, as stated in Chapter 7, the selection of the B1 type bogie for Thompson's Pacifics without working out the design characteristics needed for a much heavier engine was a major error. The fault was never discovered in the Thompson Pacifics because it was assumed that the alarming 'yawing' motion, mentioned by K. R. M. Cameron in Chapter 8, was mainly due to the flexing of the frames ahead of the outside cylinders caused by the weakness in the long gap between the bogie and the leading coupled wheels. This was, indeed, a major contributory factor; but because it concealed the weakness of the side control springs the Peppercorn Pacifics inherited an entirely unsuitable bogie. The result was that the bogie might have little centring effect on straight track, the engine being guided mainly by its leading coupled wheels. As regards the stopping of the side to side movement when the engine hit a curve, Harrison compares this to the effect 'experienced when driving a Ford car fitted with transverse front suspension (as were models of about 20 years ago) which rolled well, and which could only be driven round a corner fast by laying the car over as it approached the corner, which tightened up the front suspension till it became very hard.'[16]

It was 12 November 1957 when No 60136 entered Doncaster Works. B. C. Symes remembers the arrival of the engine. He writes:[17]

'I do not recall any official complaint being received in the Doncaster drawing office about the riding of the A1s. However, there must have been something as one of the engines was brought in for examination and re-setting of the valves, and it was then indicated by the Darlington people, who found that the IHP developed by the middle cylinder was much greater on the back stroke than the front. This was found to have been caused by the frames expanding forwards and increasing the back port opening; and the expansion allowance on the valve spindle made things worse! Accordingly the allowance on the centre valve spindle was abolished. It was decided that this unexpected fault in the steam distribution did not affect the riding, which is not surprising. So far as I know nothing further was done, so the riding cannot have been too bad! There were, or so I was told, unexpected lurches at the back end, but I never experienced them. Of course engines were normally new or newly repaired when we rode on them; though I once was on a V2 (express to Grantham) in a run down condition and I could only keep on the seat by putting an arm through the side window and gripping the outside hand rail! I think the engines as a whole suffered by comparison with the smooth riding A4s, and there would have been no grumbles by men from "Britannias" or even GN Atlantics.'

The practice of allowing for valve spindle expansion was not followed by Darlington, so that the A1 Pacifics, Nos 60130-52, built at Darlington had their valves set differently from those of the Doncaster built engines, though this was altered at their first Doncaster 'shopping'. At Doncaster the valve events were first set as near as possible to the theoretical figures, and then all three valve spindles were brought back $\frac{1}{32}$in to allow for their linear expansion when they got hot.[18]

K. R. M. Cameron, who was District Motive Power Superintendent at Kings Cross about 1951-3 and at Edinburgh from about 1955, had a great admiration for the Peppercorn Pacifics. He says:[19]

'The Peppercorn A2, which had the same rigid wheelbase as a Thompson A2/3 had the distance between the bogie centre and the leading coupled axle reduced by no less than 2ft 7in, and this may have been the reason for the better riding of this batch. Other factors could have been the longer connecting rods of the A2. So far as the A4 was concerned vis-a-vis the A1, I personally was not aware of any marked difference in the riding of them.

'The final development of the A1 was a very fine machine. We always used this type for Royal trains, and I would have been quite happy to have had a main line express stud of Peppercorn A1s. My experience of the A2 was more limited, but in a negative sense it may be said that they were all right because we did not hear many complaints about them.'

There seems to be no doubt that when the Peppercorn Pacifics had been fitted with bogies having the new side control springs, their riding was comparable with that of any other express locomotives in the country. In performance the double chimney engines were unsurpassed. J. F. Harrison rates them very high indeed, and, with his experience at the head of locomotive affairs at Doncaster and Derby, and as Chief Mechanical Engineer British Railways, his opinion is entitled to a great deal of respect. He writes as follows:[20]

'I think it is right to claim that the Peppercorn A1s were the best express passenger locomotives ever to run in this country. The word "best" needs defining. It is not, as so often seems the case, a question *only* of the ability of a locomotive to pull this or that weight of train at a known speed, or of the amount of coal burnt per train mile in doing so, or even of the maximum horsepower developed in this performance; all these factors are relevant, but at the time of Nationalisation differences recorded in respect of them by locomotives of the constituent companies were marginal, and from these figures alone one cannot draw any real conclusion as to which class of locomotive was the "best".

'The factor which is always omitted, largely because no one, official or otherwise, had any figures to prove the case one way or another, was the cost of shop and shed maintenance to both engine and boiler. However, the British Railways Board eventually decided that the collection of shop and shed maintenance costs should be assessed on a common basis. When the figures were finally produced the LNER A1s were found to be the cheapest of all the large express locomotives — despite the fact that the expensive water softening costs of the London Midland and the Southern Regions were not included, though they affected materially the costs of boiler repair and tended to increase permanent way costs because of the effect of the automatic blow-down on the ballast. The cost of the LNE water softening carried out on the GN/NE main line was comparatively negligible, but had expensive water softening treatment been installed, I would have expected the costs of boiler repair to have been much lower than they actually were.

'In my Presidential address to the Institution of Locomotive Engineers in 1961 I said: "In 1949 Doncaster produced, under the guidance of the late A. H. Peppercorn, five Pacific locomotives (part of an order for 50) having boilers pressed at 250psi, roller bearing axleboxes, and with separate valve gear drive to the middle cylinder, which we thought were the kind of locomotives Sir Nigel Gresley would have designed, had be been alive, to meet the changing conditions of maintenance. They were intended to give a better performance than any previous Pacific, to be cheaper to maintain, and to run an increased mileage per annum and between general repairs. These five locomotives, Nos 60153/54/55/56/57, have now been in service for exactly 12 years during which they have run 4.8 million miles; one in fact having just completed 1,000,000 miles or 228 miles for every calendar day since leaving Doncaster as a new engine. The average miles between "shopping" is 120,000, and these figures compare with figures given by Mr Bond in his paper to this Institution in 1953 showing the

best LNE mileage in those days as 93,363 with an average mileage of 80,000. The total miles run by the 50 engines (including the five roller bearing engines) since new is 48 million, an average of 202 miles per calendar day; figures which I know cannot be approached by any steam locomotive class in this country. I will refer to this figure later in my address. When one realises that these locomotives are better than the A4 class, examples of which took part in the Interchange trials in 1948, and which attained the best coal and water consumption figures per drawbar hp/hr, one realises that these later locomotives were, and in fact still are, perhaps the finest steam locomotives in the world.'

The distribution and use of the Peppercorn Pacifics are perhaps of some interest. Early in 1949 the A2s were allocated as follows: New England five, York four, Gateshead four, Heaton one, and Haymarket one. However, because the A2/2 (ex-P2) class locomotives were performing so unsatisfactorily in Scotland, five A2s were sent there to work the summer services of 1949 and were divided between Aberdeen and Dundee. Of these, two came from New England and three from Gateshead. In 1950 all the A2/2s were taken away from Scotland and replaced by five more A2s, so that Scotland then had all but four of them. In Scotland the A2s used primarily on the express passenger services between Edinburgh and Aberdeen, a route on which their great power and rapid acceleration could be used to advantage.

No 60532 *Blue Peter*, which was withdrawn at the end of 1966, was bought privately in 1968. It was then given an overhaul and was repainted in LNER apple green.

As soon as the A1s became available they were put immediately on to the heaviest main line expresses, replacing V2s which had of necessity been working many of these trains owing to the shortage of suitable engines. The V2s returned to fast goods and replaced to GN and NE Atlantics from the lighter main line passenger workings.

The A1s did not initially work north of Edinburgh and they were allocated as follows: Kings Cross eight, Grantham four, Doncaster five, Copley Hill five, York six, Gateshead twelve, Heaton four, and Haymarket five. In 1951 all the A4s were allocated to Kings Cross and the A1s were removed from there, the new allocations being: Grantham ten, Copley Hill ten, Ardsley two, York five, Gateshead fourteen, Heaton three, Haymarket three, and Polmadie two. Later, as we have seen, Kings Cross got them back again.[21]

One of the finest performances by an A1 that C. J. Allen ever knew was in November 1958, when No 60140 *Balmoral* was substituted at a moment's notice for a Type 4, 2,000hp diesel locomotive that had failed at York on the up afternoon 'Talisman'. The train consisted of nine coaches, weighing 325 tons gross, which was practically the same as that of the prewar 'Coronation'. *Balmoral* did rather better than the 'Coronation's' point to point timings. The 'Coronation' passed York without stopping and was booked to run from there to Kings Cross in 162 minutes. The A1 started from York and ran to Kings Cross in the net time of 158 minutes, reaching a speed of 100½mph at Essendine.[22]

A2 Pacific No 525 was not only the first of the Peppercorn Pacifics to be completed, it was also the last locomotive to be built for the LNER before Nationalisation. Sir Ronald Matthews, Chairman of the LNER, decided that the engine should be named after Peppercorn. The naming ceremony took place at Marylebone's No 4 platform. The Chairman, after paying a tribute to the Company's last CME, unveiled the nameplate which was inscribed *A. H. Peppercorn*. After a short speech in reply, Peppercorn mounted the footplate and, amidst ribald doubt from his brother railway officers about the engine's ability to move at all, drove it to the end of the platform and back.[23]

Shortly after Nationalisation, Peppercorn, having alighted from a train, walked along the platform, according to his custom, to see the engine and talk to the footplatemen. The engine was No 525, and he asked the crew what they thought of it. Not knowing who he was, the fireman replied: 'You pick up the bloody shovel when you start and you don't put it down again till you get to your destination!' Peppercorn delighted to tell this story against himself.[24]

When he came to retire at the end of 1949, Peppercorn, shy as always, wanted his farewell party to be a quiet affair. J. F. Harrison and his other principal officers were determined, however, to show their appreciation of their much loved chief in a fitting manner. After the dinner and the toasts, Harrison asked Peppercorn to turn round. He then pulled a curtain to reveal a beautiful model of No 525 *A. H. Peppercorn*. Peppercorn returned to his wife with the tears running down his face, saying, 'They got me, Pat!'[25]

Peppercorn's widow, the present Mrs Mather, showed this perfectly made model to the author. There is one difference from No 525 in that the model has a double chimney. Harrison had this put on deliberately because the last of the A2s had been built with a double chimney, and it had been such a success that it was expected that all the other A2s would get double chimneys eventually.

Notes

 1 B. C. Symes, letter to the author
 2 J. F. Harrison, letter to the author
 3 ibid
 4 ibid
 5 ibid
 6 The Railway Correspondence & Travel Society; *Locomotives of the LNER* Part 2A, pp182f
 7 ibid, pp192f
 8 ibid
 9 B. C. Symes, op cit
10 R. C. Bond, conversation with the author
11 Harrison, op cit
12 P. N. Townend, letter to the author
13 T. C. B. Miller, letter to the author
14 Townend, op cit
15 Harrison, op cit
16 ibid
17 Symes, op cit
18 RCTS, op cit, pp192f
19 K. R. M. Cameron, letter to the author
20 Harrison, op cit
21 RCTS, op cit, pp190, 200-201
22 Cecil J. Allen; *British Pacific Locomotives*; Ian Allan Ltd, 1962, pp106f
23 George Dow; *British Steam Horses*; Phoenix House, 1950, pp49-55
24 Mrs Mather, conversation with the author
25 ibid

Left: A2 class Pacific No 525
A. H. Peppercorn. / *E. R. Wethersett*

Below left: Class A2 single-chimney
Pacific No 60528 *Tudor Minstrel*
leaving Aberdeen on a train to
Edinburgh in April 1954.
/ *J. Robertson*

Top right: A2 60529 *Pearl Diver* with
an up meat train on the Tay Bridge in
1952. / *E. R. Wethersett*

Centre right: A2 No 60539 *Bronzino*
with unlipped double chimney near
the England/Scotland border beyond
Berwick with a down express in July
1952. / *E. R. Wethersett*

Below: A2 class Pacific No 60539
Bronzino with Kylchap double
blastpipe and chimney. / *D. J. Dipple*

Far left, top: A2 class Pacific No 60536 *Trimbush* at Prestonpans with the 9.10am Glasgow to Newcastle train in June 1952. / *E. R. Wethersett*

Far left, bottom: A2 Pacific No 60532 *Blue Peter* climbing to Whitrope summit with an Edinburgh to Carlisle special train on 8 October 1966. / *D. E. Gouldthorp*

Left: A1 class Pacific No 60124 *Kenilworth* on 'The Heart of Midlothian' express. / *Ian Allan Library*

Below: A1 No 60116 (un-named) heads the down 'Tees-Tyne Pullman' near Marshmoor. / *E. R. Wethersett*

Bottom: A1 No 60131 *Osprey* at the head of the down 'Flying Scotsman' taking water at Wiske Moor troughs in August 1951. Peppercorn Pacific matched by Thompson coaches. / *E. R. Wethersett*

Above: A1 No 60119 *Patrick Stirling* is smartly turned out as it comes up to Woolmer Green with the London-bound 'Yorkshire Pullman' in May 1952. / *E. R. Wethersett*

Right: Class A1 Pacific No 60127 *Wilson Worsdell* works hard on Cockburnspath bank with the up 'Queen of Scots' in March 1958. / *W. J. V. Anderson*

Below right: A1 Pacific No 60160 *Auld Reekie* leaving Motherwell with the 9.50am train from Euston to Perth. / *M. Bryce*

128

12. Locomotives under Peppercorn and Harrison

The period covered by this chapter extends from July 1946 until July 1951, when J. F. Harrison left Doncaster to become head of locomotive affairs in the London Midland Region of British Railways. This was the effective end of a locomotive practice which had stretched unbroken through the Great Northern and subsequent London & North Eastern eras since the day when Patrick Stirling had arrived at Doncaster 85 years before. The first engine for British Railways, the Pacific No 70000 *Britannia*, was built at Crewe in 1951 and the last engine of LNER design, a B1 4-6-0, was turned out from Doncaster the following year.

Thompson's renumbering scheme was mentioned briefly in Chapter 8, and this scheme was completed, as already stated, under Peppercorn on 18 January 1947. The basis of the scheme was that the number of each engine should indicate its type and its traffic function. The numbering of locomotives in the pre-Grouping companies had been haphazard and the alterations after the formation of the LNER had done nothing to make it more systematic. The first step in 1923 had been to add a letter as a suffix to existing numbers: for North British engines B, for Great Central C, for North Eastern D, for Great Eastern E, for Great Northern N, and for Great North of Scotland S. (It will be noticed that the letter chosen was the initial of an element of the old title, except in the case of the North Eastern locomotives which were allotted the D of their Darlington Works,

or from their earliest component, the Stockton & Darlington Railway.)

This numbering was replaced in 1924 by a system which is explained in the following instruction issued by the Chief Assistant Mechanical Engineer at Darlington, which was representative of similar instructions issued at the other works:

'It has been arranged that the numbering of locomotives should be: Existing stock: NE Section to retain present numbers (H&B engines to be renumbered). Other sections to add thousands to existing numbers as follows:
GN 3 thousand
GC 5 thousand
GNS vacant numbers at end of GC Section — this question to be settled between Mr Thom and Mr Heywood
GE 7 thousand
NB 9 thousand
Example: GN engine 300 would become 3300 and 1300 would become 4300.

'This will mean that there will be no necessity to retain the suffixes lettered on any locomotive in the future. It will also mean that the H&B engines will have to be renumbered entirely and I enclose a statement showing the present and future numbering to be adopted.

'The engines will be renumbered as they pass through the works for repairs and an advice of all alterations to this section's engines will be sent to you.'[1]

Even though there was obviously no bigoted adherence to the niceties of English grammar in the office of the Chief Assistant Mechanical Engineer Darlington, the meaning of the instruction is clear.

The result of the discussions between Thom and Heywood (Great Central and North British respectively) was that the GNS engines had 6800 added to their existing numbers. The NER engines kept their original numbers because that company contributed the largest number of locomotives to the common stock.

New engines constructed during the Gresley regime were given numbers from gaps in the above allotments, so that there was little advance towards a logical system.

The Thompson scheme of 1943 was, indeed, the first real attempt on the London & North Eastern Railway at a systematic numeral organisation, and it entailed renumbering the entire locomotive fleet. Blocks of numbers were allotted to the various categories as follows:

1-999	Pacifics and V2 class 2-6-2s
1000-1999	Passenger and mixed traffic tender engines of 4-6-0 and 2-6-0 types
2000-2999	Atlantic and 4-4-0 passenger tender engines
3000-3999	2-8-0 and 0-8-0 tender freight engines
4000-5999	0-6-0 tender freight engines
6000-6999	Electric locomotives
7000-7999	Passenger tank engines
8000-8999	Shunting tank engines
9000-9999	Mixed traffic and freight tank engines

(One noteworthy coincidence of the renumbering was that the B12 4-6-0s of the old Great Eastern Railway got their pre-Grouping numbers back!)

After Nationalisation LNER engines at first bore the letter E as a prefix to their numbers, but this only continued for about six weeks. Early in March 1948 British Railways announced that 60000 would be added to the ex-LNER engines in replacement of the prefix.[2]

During 1946 nine of Thompson's A2/3 class Pacifics were built, and also another 78 of the B1 class 4-6-0s. In that year, too, a number of engines of non-LNER design were taken into stock. In 1944 construction had started in LNER Works of Sir William Stanier's LMS type 2-8-0s, which had been adopted as a Ministry of Supply standard for military use. These remained on the LMS stock list, though retained by the LNER on loan, but, curiously, 25 built at the Southern Railway's Brighton Works were taken into the LNER stock as Class O6. However, in 1945 18 more of these engines were built at Doncaster and Darlington for the LNER and another 25 in 1946.

But the most massive acquisition in 1946 was the purchase from the Ministry of Supply of 275 of the locomotives built during the war for the use of the Army overseas. Of these, 190 were the so-called 'Austerity' 2-8-0s designed by R. A. Riddles for the Ministry of Supply — simple robust engines with a parallel boiler and round-top firebox — which were taken into LNER stock as Class O7. They were not new to the LNER, for 350 had been lent to the company whilst awaiting shipment overseas. They had proved extremely successful, so much so that O. S. Nock, in his book *Steam Locomotives*, quotes a very senior railway officer at York who loved North Eastern engines as saying that the 'WDs' were by far the best freight engines they had ever had. The Austerity 2-8-0s had some relation to the LMS 2-8-0s because the outline scheme had been got out by F. G. Carrier, a draughtsman who was section leader in the development and design branch of the Derby drawing office.[3]

The other Ministry of Supply engines purchased were 74 0-6-0 saddle tanks which became LNER Class J94. Some of them were delivered direct from the makers, the Hunslet Engine Company. These engines were derived from Hunslet's very fine little standard shunter, but with certain modifications that Riddles had asked should be incorporated to make them suitable for mass construction in the light of the materials available.[4] Because of the purchase of these two classes the construction of the more expensive O1 2-8-0s and J50 0-6-0 medium shunting tanks was unnecessary.

As we have seen, the first Peppercorn Pacific appeared in 1947 and all of them, both A2s and A1s, were in service before the end of 1949. The large number of 186 B1 4-6-0s were built in 1947, and the last six of Thompson's A2/3 class Pacifics. During this, the LNER's last year, though it was as short of funds as ever, the emphasis on cutting expenditure, which had restricted locomotive construction during the whole of its prewar existence, was paradoxically replaced by anxiety over the difficulties of getting needed engines built and of obtaining the materials necessary for their manufacture.

Fifty-nine of Thompson's L1 class 2-6-4 tanks made an apparently belated appearance during 1948, for the solitary prototype had been built in 1945. Sixty-eight more of the B1s made their appearance, and these most useful engines were working traffic all over the lines of the old LNER.

So far the only K1 had been Thompson's rebuilding in 1945 of a K4, but it was such a successful engine that an order was placed for 70 new ones of the same design. Sixty-one were delivered in 1949 and the final nine in the following year. Although a two-cylinder engine, the K1 was still, of course, primarily a Gresley design.[5]

As the light shunting tank engine envisaged in Thompson's standardisation scheme had not as yet been designed, there was a most interesting decision to adopt the 0-6-0 side tank engine which had been built for the North Eastern Railway by Wilson Worsdell, as Class E1, as long ago as 1898. The selection of a 50-year old class to meet a modern requirement, with virtually no modification, must be almost unique in locomotive annals. The Great Western 0-6-0 dock shunting pannier tank engines of 1934 come to mind, because they were derived from the 1873 engines of the Cornwall Mineral Railway, but they were copies (except for having pannier instead of side tanks), of a modernised version of the Cornish engines produced by H. Holcroft in 1910.[6] Twenty-eight of these little North Eastern engines were ordered, of which 15 were delivered in 1949, five in 1950 and the remaining eight in 1951. These last eight were fitted with vacuum ejectors to enable them to work coaching stock and fitted freight vehicles, but all were Class J72. The first of them was completed at Darlington Works in October 1949, 51 years after the first of the original batch had been built there.[7] J. F. Harrison says that they were grand little engines — most economical and effective.

There were 15 more L1 tanks in 1949, and the order for these indifferent engines was completed with 25 more in 1950. Eighteen B1s appeared in 1949, 24 more in 1950, 19 in 1951, and a final batch of seven in 1952.[8]

The rapid increase in the number of B1s resulted in the scrapping of most of the pre-Grouping engines which had been working the light expresses and secondary passenger services over so many years. These engines had had an extended life due to the war and their age had made their maintenance increasingly expensive. There was a wholesale withdrawal of the impressive-looking but disappointing Great Central 4-6-0s; all of them were scrapped during the years 1947 to 1950, including the solitary Thompson rebuild of one of the four-cylinder 'Lord Faringdons'. The last of the classic Great Northern Atlantics went in 1950, as did also the shapely Great Central Atlantics; but all the North Eastern Atlantics had gone by 1948. In 1950 the last of the Great Central D9 4-4-0s, employed on the Cheshire Lines Liverpool-Manchester expresses, were withdrawn, and after 1951 the only North Eastern 4-6-0s left were the B16s.[9]

Nevertheless, it is astonishing how many locomotives of the pre-Grouping companies were still running when J. F. Harrison departed from Doncaster. The principal classes by which the old Companies were still represented were as follows:

North Eastern Railway

A7 three-cylinder mineral 4-6-2 tank engines of 1910; A8 4-6-2 tank engines, rebuilt from Raven's 4-4-4 tanks of 1913; Raven's three-cylinder 4-6-0 mixed traffic engines of LNER class B16, in their original condition and also as rebuilt by Gresley and Thompson; the famous old R class 4-4-0s of the NER, first built in 1899, which became Class D20 of the LNER; the three classes of the capable 0-8-0 mineral engines, comprising both the two-cylinder and three-cylinder varieties; five classes of 0-6-0 goods engines; and a large number of tank engines of different types.

Great Northern Railway

K2 two-cylinder and K3 three-cylinder 2-6-0s; the original O1 class two-cylinder 2-8-0s, reclassified as O3, and the three-cylinder 2-8-0s of Class O2; Ivatt's and Gresley's N1 and N2 0-6-2 tank engines; Ivatt's 4-4-2 tanks; and 0-6-0 goods engines by Stirling, Ivatt and Gresley.

Great Eastern Railway

The grand B12 4-6-0 engines in both their original and rebuilt forms; the D15 'Claud' 4-4-0s, the Gresley rebuild of the 'Claud Hamiltons' as D16/3 and the D16/1s and D16/2s, which were the Hill 'Super-Clauds' with Belpaire fireboxes; four classes of 0-6-0 goods engines, including the J20 which was the nost powerful engine of this type on the LNER; the N7 0-6-2 tank which was adopted and multiplied by Gresley; Holden's mixed traffic 2-4-0s of LNER Class E4; and a number of 2-4-2 and 0-6-0 tank engine classes.

Great Central Railway

'Director' class 4-4-0s, of which more were built under Gresley for Scotland; the famous O4 class 2-8-0 mineral engines, of which a number had been rebuilt by Thompson as O1; 0-6-0 goods engines, including the 'Pom-Poms', which became a Thompson standard; the Q1 class 0-8-0 mineral engines, some of which were rebuilt by Thompson as his standard heavy shunting engines; and the successful A5 4-6-2 tank engine.

North British Railway

The earlier and later 'Scott' class 4-4-0s; three 'Intermediate' 4-4-0 classes, of which the latest were the 'Glens', the best of all North British passenger engines; J35 0-6-0 goods engines; and 0-6-0 and 0-6-2 tank engines.

Great North of Scotland Railway

Pickersgill and Johnson D40 and D41 4-4-0 engines; and sundry 0-4-2 tanks.

It is an impressive list, which no other British railway could equal, but the presence of so many nostalgic reminders of pre-Grouping days was largely due to the LNER's perennial shortage of money.

In 1946 the LNER had announced its intention of painting all its engines in the prewar green livery, but Nationalisation arrived before much progress could be made on this admirable scheme. However, the small tank engines used as station pilots at Liverpool Street, York, Newcastle, and Edinburgh were painted green and kept spotlessly clean and polished.[10]

It is worth considering what would have happened in the LNER locomotive world if there had been no Nationalisation. J. F. Harrison would, of course, have succeeded Peppercorn as CME, and would presumably have remained so, at least until 1966 (the date that he retired from the equivalent post on British Railways). Harrison says[11] that because the LNER was so desperately short of money he does not think that there would have been much new rolling stock. In common with general opinion on the LNER, he would have liked a more powerful steam locomotive, capable of hauling 500 tons at average speeds of 70mph or above between Newcastle and London and to intermediate places. The locomotive that Harrison would have designed would have been a 4-8-2 with a round-top boiler pressed at 275psi, three cylinders 21in diameter by 26in stroke, driving wheels of 6ft 4in diameter, caprotti valve gear (independent to each cylinder), automatic stoker, single-shot lubrication wherever possible, and a corridor tender. The automatic stoker was a most interesting addition — particularly as Chapelon had shown (contrary to prevailing British opinion) on his 240P class 2-8-0s that by lengthening the brick arch to burn the small coal particles, which would otherwise have been ejected, the consumption of heat was only greater (as compared with hand firing) by the 10% needed to work the stoker.[12] As regards other engines, Harrison would have continued the B1s and K1s, which had proved exceedingly satisfactory in service, and would have built more 0-6-0 side tank engines.

Harrison's three-cylinder simple 4-8-2, however, would have only been a stage towards a much more revolutionary engine. If it had been successful he would have designed another 4-8-2, but this would have been a four-cylinder compound with the high pressure of 400psi and a water-tube firebox. The principal reason for this very high pressure was so that the low-pressure cylinders could be kept relatively small, because four cylinders, even in a simple expansion locomotive, were always tight transversely to loading gauge. It is a very great pity that such an engine was never built. A. Chapelon has always maintained that a four-cylinder compound similar to his outstanding 240P class 4-8-0 could have been built inside the British loading gauge, and one of these engines developed 3,600 equivalent drawbar horsepower. There was every possibility, therefore, that Harrison's proposed compound would have developed more power at the drawbar than do the 'Deltic' diesels — themselves the most powerful diesel locomotives in the country.

Harrison was unable to build this great engine, but he did get a chance to apply some of his ideas when, as Mechanical and Electrical Engineer of the London Midland Region, he was responsible for building No 71000 *Duke of Gloucester* at Derby. This, the only Class 8 Pacific of British Railways, had an interesting background. One of Stanier's 'Princess' class Pacifics, No 6202, had been built with a turbine drive, and it was rebuilt after Nationalisation with the conventional reciprocating motion. Not long after rebuilding, the engine (now No 46202) was completely wrecked in the bad smash at Harrow in October 1952. This gave R. A. Riddles the opportunity to ask and obtain authority to build a new Class 8 Pacific with which running experience might be gained for a future building of standard Class 8 express engines.

Riddles, like Harrison, thought highly of Caprotti valve gear ever since, under the direction of H. P. M. Beames, he had fitted it to some of the LNWR 'Claughton' class 4-6-0s. He had felt that if the theory of smooth straight passages for steam was right, then one could hardly improve on a poppet valve, with full exhaust opening at all positions of the reversing gear. Since the mechanical troubles previously experienced had been largely overcome, it was well worth trying, and the manufacturers were most anxious that another trial should be made. It was not practicable to provide two cylinders large enough for the power required and Riddles chose three, rather than four, on account of the more even turning moment. When these decisions had been made the task of detailed design was turned over to the Derby drawing office and Harrison became responsible for building the engine.[13] The results which Harrison achieved with that gear on the *Duke of Gloucester* are recorded in Chapter 9.

Like Chapelon, Harrison believed strongly in streamlined steam passages. He writes:[14] 'It has always seemed to me that no one took much notice of this very obvious way to improve steam flow, and when I built the *Duke of Gloucester* I not only insisted on meticulous matching of the passage ways through the outside cylinders to the exhaust pipe orifice, but that the passage ways should be ground and polished.' Another Harrison feature was the middle big end. Thompson had ascribed the middle big end heating on Gresley's Pacifics to the excessive travel at speed of the middle valve, and this suited his general condemnation of the two-to-one valve gear. The weakness, says Harrison, was, however, due to the stretch and flexibility of the strap. It was very difficult to ensure tight big end bolts when the strap could both flex and stretch. 'The only really satisfactory middle big end I know', he adds, 'was the one I fitted to the *Duke of Gloucester*, being exceptionally strong, with a large easily adjustable cotter and hefty bolts. At no time did this give any trouble.' This is endorsed by E. S. Cox, who says[15] that Harrison had long been interested in the subject and that it was under his personal supervision that the fork type big end used was worked out. He comments particularly on the exceptionally robust clip closing the jaws of the rod and the serrated locking device for the cotter, which permitted exactly the correct degree of tightness to be retained and locked up against involuntary movement.

Of *Duke of Gloucester's* performance, however, Cox comments that although the engine portion proved superb and showed a cylinder efficiency unmatched by any other simple expansion engine in the world, the boiler performance and efficiency was markedly inferior at high outputs.[16] To this Harrison replies:[17]

'In so far as the latter is concerned, it became apparent in its early life that this "one-off" locomotive, working alongside "Duchesses", etc had to be fired in a way that was quite foreign to an LMS-designed boiler. The latter was fired all over the firegrate and right up to the top of the firehole itself, whereas 71000 had to be fired exactly like an A4 — that is, regularly into the back corners and level with the bottom of the firehole door. When the A4s worked between Glasgow and Carlisle the same trouble was experienced; the men said that they were no good, until they had been taught how to fire them. When 71000 was put on the Test Plant it was fired in a similar manner to all LMS engines and consequently did not burn the coal properly — because it was not fired properly. The engine had so many good points about it that the pity was that it never got properly evaluated.'

Riddles endorses this. He says that the engine was never given a fair chance. Like Ivatt's prototype diesels, she was the victim of a link system. She required an entirely different technique from the LMS 'Duchesses'. A driver might have the new Pacific one day and then LMS types for the next fortnight or more. Riddles had personal experience of No 71000, for after he had retired from the railway he drove her himself from Rugby to Crewe, picking up the six minutes which the driver, unfamiliar with the engine, had lost between Euston and Rugby.[18]

It seems a pity that No 71000 was not tried on the Eastern Region in the same link as A4s, when there might have been no reservations about the engine's excellence. Indeed, Harrison says that the engine went for a time to the Western Region, where she came under S. O. Ell, in charge of the Swindon test plant, and worked, amongst other trains, the 'Cornish Riviera Express' to his entire satisfaction. One cannot help wishing that *Duke of Gloucester* had been fitted with the Kylchap double exhaust, rather than the plain double blast pipe and chimney, considering the great improvement that the Kylchap had made to LNER engines.

Harrison says[19] that the LNER (or rather its British Railways descendants) changed very reluctantly to diesel power. They remembered only too well the proposal for a 'Flying Hamburger'-type train, which analysis eventually showed could not provide a service of the speed that was required; whereas practical trials showed that steam could: the A4 was the result. In addition, a visiting American railway officer had remarked on how lucky the English were in not being plagued with diesels and certain other denizens of the United States. Nevertheless, when Ivatt was developing his 10000 and 10001 diesel-electrics for the LMS, the LNER felt that they must keep a careful watch, and do better than the rival railway if diesels became a going concern. During Harrison's time at Doncaster no designs for diesel locomotives were prepared. The real start of dieselisation more or less coincided with Harrison's appointment as Chief Mechanical Engineer, British Railways, in October 1958. Of this period he writes:[20]

'The LNER, having always believed in a big engine policy (and *how* right they were), took over the prototype "Deltic" and found the power much to their liking; so much so that the "Deltics" (maintained by English Electric) worked the East Coast main line. Here I came into the picture. Our experience with the German high speed engines made me very wary over the "Deltic", and R. C. Bond held the same view. We both liked the medium-speed English Electric engines (really good and reliable). We could not see that an engine from a motor torpedo boat would stand up to railway use for 20-25 years on both freight and passenger work, and I think we were right. Certainly the proposed high speed trains have high-speed engines, but they are virtually multi-unit passenger trains and will not do any freight work. Further, it would be unreasonable to suppose that improvements in high-speed engine reliability have not occurred during the last 15 years. The LNER men liked the "Deltic" because it was so easily master of the job and could in fact top Stoke summit at 90mph.

'The British Transport Commission were diesel-mad at this time and insisted on buying far too many diesels too soon, before either footplate staff or, more particularly, maintenance staff were properly trained. It took, I would say, nearly 10 years for the fitters of steam days to be properly retrained to maintain diesel locomotives.'

Electrification in the years before Nationalisation did not appeal to Harrison, because he thought it too expensive to justify itself; particularly as projects were related to the medium voltage dc system, rather than the high voltage ac, which S. B. Warder eventually prevailed on the BTC to adopt. Electrification, indeed, at that time was little considered in the BTC's future policy. In fact, the policy statement, which contained practically no plans for additional electrification, was already at the printers when Warder finally persuaded the BTC to electrify the Manchester-Crewe line with a high-voltage ac system. As Harrison says, he deserves full credit for forcing the BTC to start high-voltage electrification against both their own views and those of the Government.

The 50 c/s ac system in Great Britain has an interesting history. In March 1951 R. A. Riddles, Member of the Railway Executive for Mechanical and Electrical Engineering (a cumbersome way of saying CME), was invited by the French SNCF to attend a demonstration at Annécy on the 50 c/s trial route between Aix-les-Bains and La Roche-sur-Furon. He took with him his Chief Electrical Engineer, S. B. Warder. Many representatives of British electrical firms were also present. Riddles was so impressed with the demonstration and with the whole concept of 50 c/s ac traction that he invited the representatives of the British firms to a cocktail party and discussed with them the possibilities of introducing this system into Great Britain. He remembered that the Railway Executive had, a little time earlier, decided to abandon electric traction on the Morecambe-Heysham line because the system, which had been installed in 1908, was

worn out, and to revert to steam operation. Accordingly he told his guests that if they would persuade their principals to supply the equipment free of charge, he would provide vehicles and facilities to try out 50 c/s on this line. The firms agreed and the electrification of the line on the new system was carried out under Warder's direction.[21]

It was only after the initial success of the Manchester-Crewe electrification that Harrison became an enthusiast for this form of rail traction, largely because, as he says, he was brain-washed by his staff, successfully led by A. H. Emerson. He continues:[22]

'They did a wonderful job from scratch, and so little has been said about the enormous difficulties encountered, particularly in the recruitment of staff. There was a great dearth of electrical engineers with a railway background who could not only undertake the engineering 'hardware', but also deal with all the railway departments affected — for the latter understood and appreciated the problems even less than a confirmed heretic like myself.'

The difficulties in training, Harrison says, were even greater than those presented by the diesels, but time was fortunately on the side of the engineers, because the Government took many years to make up their minds over electrification and use was made of the waiting period to train a number of very young men in the construction of the necessary equipment and to evolve suitable maintenance practices and schedules. Compared with dieselisation, therefore, electrification 'went with a bang' and was successful from the start.

Harrison adds: 'Too little credit has been given to A. H. Emerson for the field work and to S. B. Warder, his Assistant Alan Broughall, and his staff for the design work. All I did was to give what encouragement I could, whilst I was at Derby, to Emerson and his boys in their creation of the initial high-voltage line from Manchester to Crewe.'

It is strange to recollect that, whilst there has not yet occurred that electrification of the East Coast route for which Sir Vincent Raven built an express passenger locomotive, an East Coast man eventually presided over the electrification of the West Coast route.

Notes

1 The Railway Correspondence & Travel Society; *Locomotives of the LNER* Part I, p30
2 ibid, pp37f
3 Colonel H. C. B. Rogers; *The Last Steam Locomotive Engineer: R. A. Riddles, C.B.E.*; George Allen & Unwin, 1970, p118
4 ibid, p124
5 RCTS, op cit, pp20-21
6 Colonel H. C. B. Rogers; *G. J. Churchward: A Locomotive Biography*; George Allen & Unwin, 1975, pp135-136
7 K. Hoole; *North Road Locomotive Works Darlington 1863-1966;* Roundhouse Books, 1967, pp62-63
8 RCTS, op cit
9 ibid, pp105f
10 H. C. Casserley; *Locomotive Cavalcade*; Author, 1952, p150
11 J. F. Harrison, letter to the author
12 Colonel H. C. B. Rogers; *Chapelon: Genius of French Steam*; Ian Allan Ltd, 1972, p36
13 Rogers; *The Last Steam Locomotive Engineers*; pp182, 189
14 Harrison, letter to the author
15 E. S. Cox; *British Railways Standard Steam Locomotives*; Ian Allan Ltd, 1966, p111
16 ibid, p128
17 Harrison, letter to the author
18 Rogers; *The Last Steam Locomotive Engineer*; pp190, 204
19 Harrison, letter to the author
20 ibid
21 Rogers; *The Last Steam Locomotive Engineer*; pp160-161
22 Harrison, letter to the author

Left: Stanier LMS type 2-8-0 as LNER Class O6 in March 1946.
/ *E. R. Wethersett*

Above: Riddles 'Austerity' 0-6-0 tank engine as LNER Class J94 No 8027 at Darlington in August 1947.
/ *E. V. Fry*

Right: Class O6 (LMS type) No 3548 coaling at York on 29 July 1947.
/ *C. C. B. Herbert*

Above: Rather an impostor in the LNER green livery which it never carried (but nonetheless convincing) preserved K1 2-6-0 No 2005 leaves Goathland for Pickering on the North York Moors Railway in April 1978. / *E. A. Parker*

Left: K1 No 62007 approaches York from the north with a freight train. / *Eric Treacy*

Top right: K1 and K4 compared: preserved K4 No 3442 leads K1 62005 into Bridlington on a railtour in March 1965. In particular notice the substitution of Darlington lines for Gresley features. / *D. Hardy*

Centre right: Postwar J72 No 69027 acts as station pilot at Newcastle Central on 21 May 1962. / *M. Mensing*

Bottom right: NER S3 class 4-6-0 No 1403, rebuilt by Thompson as B16/3. / *P. Ransome-Wallis*

Above: B16/3 4-6-0 No 61448 near Castle Howard in August 1951. / *E. R. Wethersett*

Right: B16/3 class 4-6-0 No 61453 leaving York on a train on 20 May 1953. / *Eric Treacy*

Below right: BR three-cylinder 4-6-0 No 71000 *Duke of Gloucester* on Crewe Bank 17 July 1954. / *H. A. Chelkey*

13. The Background to the Achievements of Thompson and Peppercorn

'The basis of the increase of power in a locomotive lies in enlarging the area of the grate and increasing the efficiency of the steam circuit; everything else being equal, the productive capacity of the boiler depends on the number of calories per second emitted in the firebox from a fuel of given calorific value and from a given thickness of fire. It is obvious therefore that this power depends on the extent of the grate . . .

'Nevertheless, the total power of the boiler does not depend only on the area of the grate. The correct funtioning of the exhaust plays a decisive part, and experience shows that when one can obtain a sufficient draught under all conditions, a boiler with a small grate area will allow greater powers to be developed than will a boiler of large dimensions but with the draught impeded by a defective exhaust . . .

'The heating surface, to which so great an importance was attached for such a long time is, however, only a secondary factor in the functioning of the locomotive.'[1]

So writes André Chapelon, that great master of steam. It is apparent that, whereas the design of the boiler is important, the figures commonly provided of its heating surface do not indicate its ability to undertake its primary task of boiling water. The three principal factors are the grate area, the efficiency of the steam circuit, and the exhaust. Of course, in addition to the efficiency of steam production and steam flow, a locomotive must behave adequately as a vehicle and be reasonably cheap both to run and to maintain.

With the above factors in mind, an opinion as to any advances in locomotive design under the regimes of Thompson and Peppercorn cannot really be made without reference to the more recent evolution of the steam locomotive. Such a study might best start with the origin and development of the type of locomotive which has figured most prominently in these pages in connection with both engineers; that is, the Pacific.

The first Pacific locomotive built in Great Britain was the famous No 111 *The Great Bear* of the Great Western Railway, designed by G. J. Churchward and completed in February 1908. It was nearly, but not quite, the first Pacific in Europe, for only a year previously the Paris-Orleans Railway had put into service the first two of a class of four-cylinder compound Pacifics with 6ft 0¾in diameter coupled wheels. Two years later there came the first of another class of almost similar Pacifics, but with larger coupled wheels having a diameter of 6ft 4¾in. The relationship between *The Great Bear* and the Paris-Orleans Pacifics was very close, because both had their origins in the same class of locomotives — the four-cylinder compound Atlantics designed by Gaston du Bousquet, Engineer-in-Chief of the Nord Railway, and Alfred de Glehn, the British-born Chief Engineer of the *Société Alsacienne de Constructions Mécaniques*. Not only the Nord, but also other French railways bought these Atlantics, and those of the PO were rather larger than the original ones built for the Nord. In 1902 Churchward ordered one of the Nord-type Atlantics to compare with his own two-cylinder simple expansion 4-6-0s, and converted one of the latter into an Atlantic to make the comparison more exact. Later he obtained authority to order two more French Atlantics, but of the larger PO type.

Though there was little to choose in performance and economy between the British and the French engines, Churchward preferred his own simple expansion type with their long lap and long travel valves. On the other hand, the compounds, with their four cylinders, divided drive, and balanced reciprocating masses, were much smoother riding than the two-cylinder engines. Churchward decided, therefore, to build a four-cylinder simple Atlantic with the same divided drive and position of the outside cylinders as used on the French compounds, the outside cylinders being beside the rear bogie wheels and the inside well forward so that the connecting rods could be of practically the same length. The result was the famous *North Star*, which was subsequently altered to the 4-6-0 wheel arrangement because Churchward, after a comparison of the two types, decided that Atlantics did not have sufficient adhesion for the steep South Devon banks.

The Paris-Orleans, whilst using the Atlantics on the main line to Bordeaux, had also felt the want of adhesion on their heavily graded line to Toulouse, and had designed a 4-6-0 which was identical with the Atlantics except for having coupled wheels of 6ft 3¾in diameter instead of 6ft 8½in.

On the Great Northern Railway, H. A. Ivatt had in 1902 built the first of his large Atlantics with parallel boiler and wide round-top firebox — a vastly different conception to the typical Churchward engine with narrow Belpaire firebox and tapered boiler. Churchward, however, liked the idea of this wide firebox. In a discussion on a paper on *American Locomotive Practice* read before the Institution of Civil Engineers on 31 March 1903, he said:

'Probably, to English locomotive engineers, the part of the paper which deals with boilers is the most interesting; especially the reasonably wide firebox which the author has described. An express engine with a similar box has just been put on the Great Northern Railway by Mr Ivatt, and I trust it will have a good trial in England. I think English locomotive engineers are within a reasonable distance of adopting it, and I am sorry that the French Atlantic engine which is to be put on the Great Western Railway is not fitted with it — but I am taking the engine as it stands.'

The du Bousquet-de Glehn Atlantics had indeed a Belpaire firebox and narrow grate. Nevertheless Churchward decided to try the wide firebox; but, since he had already decided that an Atlantic lacked adhesion, the engine would have to be a Pacific, and so was conceived *The Great Bear*, with a grate area of 41.79sq ft. The engine had too heavy an axle loading at that time for any of the Great Western main lines except that between Paddington and Bristol. There was therefore ample time to test this prototype locomotive before the civil engineering work, already in progress, had brought the Plymouth and Birmingham main lines up to the standard needed for a fleet of Pacifics. The tests, whch were most detailed, were conducted by the 'Experimental Gang' of the Swindon drawing office. There were a number of teething troubles, as one would expect in such a revolutionary engine. There were complaints, in particular, about steaming troubles (as were later to be made about the *Duke of Gloucester*) until firemen found out how to fire the unfamiliar wide firebox. The big boiler with its wide Belpaire firebox was a notable feature. Churchward did not like combustion chambers, so the tubes were of the unusual length of 23ft, but this was compensated by a tube diameter of 2½in, instead of the 2in of the 'Stars'. The engine was the first to have the de Glehn bogie, used on the French Atlantics, which subsequently became standard on the Great Western, the LMS, and the British Railways locomotives. The arrangement of cylinders and motion was the same as that of the 'Stars'. The one weak part of the engine was the radial truck with inside bearings, because the axleboxes overheated due to the difficulty of lubricating them and to the exposure of their surfaces to dust from the ashpans and grit from the track.

World War I interrupted both the tests and the engineering work on the main lines, and before normal conditions could be resumed on the railways Churchward retired. His successor, C. B. Collett, had no use for *The Great Bear* and scrapped it. Nevertheless, had Churchward remained, the need for increased power on the Great Western, which he undoubtedly foresaw, would have probably taken the form of a Pacific class, modified in the light of experience with *The Great Bear*. As stated in Chapter 8, Churchward would have welcomed the opportunity to try his engine on the Great Northern main line.

It was the search for greater power which led the Paris-Orleans Company to build its two classes of compound Pacifics. They had the same arrangement of cylinders as the Atlantics and an appearance somewhat similar to that of *The Great Bear*, even including the inside bearings of the trailing truck! One class, intended to replace the 4-6-0s, had coupled wheels of 6ft 0¾in, whilst the other, replacing the Atlantics on the Bordeaux main line, had 6ft 4¾in coupled wheels. Both classes had a Belpaire firebox which was wide and shallow at the bank and deep and narrow at the back. This design is called in France 'trapezoidal' (ie irregularly quadrilateral) and was adopted by engineers who wanted to keep the advantages of the deep grate.[2] It is conceivable that there was too much of a rush over the design of these Pacifics, because they did not provide that increase in power over their predecessors that had been expected. Indicator diagrams of cylinder performance showed throttling of steam at admission to the cylinders, high back pressure at the exhaust, and a considerable drop in pressure in the intermediate receiver between high-pressure and low-pressure cylinders. None of these things would have happened in a Churchward-designed steam circuit. It is a pity *The Great Bear* could not have been tried out between Paris and Bordeaux!

There was yet a third railway which had Pacifics that were descendants of the du Bousquet-de Glehn Atlantics. In 1914 M. Asselin, then head of locomotive affairs on the Nord Railway, designed some four-cylinder compound Pacifics that were not in fact built because of the outbreak of World War I. In 1923 these engines were built, though with a slightly smaller firebox than the original design, and appeared in service as the famous 'Super-Pacifics' of the Nord. They adhered more closely than did the PO Pacifics to the original Atlantic design, because they had a

Belpaire firebox with a narrow grate and the exceptional length of 11ft 8in. But although the grate area was only 37.7sq ft, A. Chapelon points out[3] that they were capable of nearly 30% greater power output than other contemporary French Pacifics. They were at the time, in fact, the finest express engines in Europe, developing up to 2,700 indicated horsepower at speed. The first batch were remarkable in having balanced slide valves instead of piston valves, but the steam circuit was extremely well designed.

From the du Bousquet-de Glehn Atlantic, then, were developed three Pacific designs. Of these, *The Great Bear* was destined to influence the design of Pacifics on the LMS and British Railways, the PO Pacifics were to provide the foundation for Chapelon's revolutionary work, and from the Nord 'Super-Pacifics' Chapelon took the boiler and firebox for his conversion of PO Pacifics into 4-8-0s.

Though perhaps slightly out of chronological order, Sir Vincent Raven's Pacifics for the North Eastern Railway might be discussed here, because they marked the end, rather than the beginning, of a development in locomotive design.

In 1911 Raven produced his handsome and capable Z class Atlantics for the North Eastern Railway, and when the last appeared in 1918 there were 50 of them. As compared with Worsdell's two-cylinder V class Atlantics, which drove on the second coupled axle, all three cylinders of the Zs drove on the leading coupled axle. One advantage claimed for this arrangement was that the outside connecting rods could be placed inside the coupling rods and therefore nearer to the wheels. The three cylinders and smokebox-supporting saddle were all in a single steel casting, and the connecting rods were all of the same length. In order that this length should be adequate, the distance between the leading coupled wheels and the rear bogie wheels was made longer than on the V Atlantics.

In 1922-3 Raven's five Pacific locomotives were turned out from Darlington Works. They were in many respects enlarged versions of the Z Atlantics, though with a wide, instead of a narrow, firebox. There was the same type of single casting for cylinders, valve chests, and smokebox saddle. All three cylinders again drove on the leading coupled axle, but the connecting rods looked somewhat short for an engine of this size; even though that extra distance between rear bogie wheels and leading coupled wheels entailed a long wheel base which in practice proved something of a handicap. There were three separate sets of Stephenson valve gear, and all inside, which produced something of a squash, to say the least, between the main bearings in the frames, and bearing lengths were inevitably restricted. The front end design was pre-Churchward, and whilst the engines were not much inferior in running to the first Gresley Pacifics in their original form, it would have been a difficult task to modernise the valve arrangements in the same way. Inevitably, of course, with their restricted bearings, they suffered from heating troubles, but they could, and did, perform the job they were designed for, though in a rather undistinguished way and at more than average fuel consumption. Churchward would have raised his eyebrows at the design in 1902, and in 1922 they were more than 20 years out of date.

The basis of Gresley's long line of Pacifics, and indeed of Thompson's and Peppercorn's too, lay in Ivatt's large boiler Atlantic of 1902. Indeed, this engine, together with Churchward's two-cylinder 4-6-0 of 1903 and his four-cylinder *North Star* of 1906, provided the foundation for all modern British express locomotive design. Churchward's approval of Ivatt's wide firebox has already been recorded, and this, together with the enormous (for the time) 5ft 6in diameter boiler, testified to Ivatt's belief that the ability of an engine to boil water was more important than the theoretical power conferred by the size of its cylinders.

Gresley's first design for a Great Northern Pacific was as early as 1915. It was anticipated that there would be a need for greater adhesion than the Atlantics could provide to work the heavier trains of the future. Other railways had been building 4-6-0s to meet this expected demand, but

Gresley wanted to retain the wide firebox which was well suited to the Great Northern's staple diet of Yorkshire coal; and so, like Churchward before him, for a similar reason, he chose a Pacific. This was to have been a four-cylinder engine with a parallel boiler of the same 5ft 6in diameter as that of the Atlantics. All four cylinders were to drive on the second coupled axle, the inside cylinder piston valves being actuated by rocking shafts from outside Walschaerts valve gear. To try out this arrangement, one of the large Atlantics was rebuilt as a four-cylinder engine. However, this Pacific never materialised.[4] Such an engine would not have incorporated any particular technical advance, and in fact, except for the cylinders, it would have been — like Raven's Pacific — a lengthened version of its Atlantic predecessor.

Gresley's first Pacific, when it did come, was a much more revolutionary engine and all subsequent Great Northern and London & North Eastern Pacifics, even Thompson's, were descended from it. It was not entirely original, but then no really great locomotive designs are; they owe their success to their creators incorporating proved practice and building on the work of other engineers before them. Like G. J. Churchward, Gresley took an intense interest in American locomotive design. In 1910 the American Locomotive Company built an experimental Pacific locomotive, No 50000. The Erie Railway tested it on express passenger trains and bought it. In 1911 the Pennsylvania Railroad ordered a similar but rather larger engine, and after testing it on service and at their Altoona plant they produced a slightly modified design, which was the prototype of their standard and very successful K4 class of Pacific express locomotives. It was a two-cylinder engine with a taper boiler and a wide Belpaire firebox with a combustion chamber. The first of the K4s appeared in 1913, and between then and 1928 no fewer than 450 were built. While the K4 class were still being built the Pennsylvania put into service a larger version with a higher boiler pressure, which was designated K5. In 1916 the K4 was described in detail in the British magazine *Engineering*, and it was probably from this article that Gresley got the idea of building a similar type of boiler.[5] But the Pacific which emerged from Doncaster was essentially Gresley's own. It was a beautifully balanced design, not only as a piece of engineering but also to look at. It was in fact one of the most handsome locomotives to be built in Great Britain or anywhere else. As subsequently modified with long-travel valves and a higher boiler pressure, it was the finest express locomotive in the country.

The next step in Pacific design came from France. In 1926 André Chapelon, then of the Research and Development Section of the Paris-Orleans Railway Design Office, designed his Kylchap exhaust, which was tested with great success on the Pacifics and other large Paris-Orleans engines. Chapelon thought that even better results could be obtained by increasing the cross-sectional area of the steam passages. He thought they should be doubled, that all sharp bends in the steam pipes should be eliminated, and that the volume of the steam chests should be increased. These measures, he considered, would reduce the losses from throttling which were occurring in the steam circuit from regulator to exhaust. But apart from the steam passages, other matters in the PO compound Pacifics demanded attention. He had measured the temperature in the intermediate receiver of one of the superheated engines and found that the degree of superheat in the low-pressure cylinders was practically nil. It was evident that if the condensation in the low-pressure group could be eliminated there would be a still further gain in efficiency. The improvement in economy of the superheated over the original saturated engines was about 20%, and this was with 300°C (572°F) of superheat; but the gain was almost entirely in the high-pressure cylinders. If the low-pressure cylinders could be made to contribute their proper share, it seemed reasonable to anticipate a further 10%. Chapelon estimated that to get this it would be necessary to raise the temperature of the superheat by 100°C (180°F) at the admission to the high-pressure cylinders. The provision of oil and castings suitable for this higher temperature presented a problem, but he managed to solve it. From these calculations Chapelon now assessed the overall improvement which could be expected from one of the compound Pacifics rebuilt in accordance with the above principles. Taking the average indicated horsepower of a superheated compound Pacific of the large-wheeled 3500 class, running at high speed, to be 1,850, he reckoned that the proposed improvements in the steam circuit would raise it by 20% to 2,200, and that the increase in superheat should add another 10%, making it 2,400. In addition, the improved draughting with the Kylchap exhaust should increase the boiler output by 25% and so raise the indicated horsepower to 3,000.

As a result of Chapelon's argument it was decided to rebuild one of the 3500 class Pacifics, and because of the high superheat envisaged, the locomotive chosen was one on which it had already been intended to try the Lentz poppet valve system, but it was thought best to retain the existing Walschaerts gear to actuate oscillating cams.

The first engine to be rebuilt was No 3566, which was about the worst of the whole class — so bad that the enginemen had nicknamed it 'Cholera' on account of its internal disorder! Due to the death of Chapelon's immediate chief and the retirement of the Engineer-in-Chief of Rolling Stock and Motive Power there were delays in the rebuilding of the engine, which did not appear from the Company's Tours Works until November 1929. As completed the engine incorporated, in addition to the improvements discussed above, an ACFI feed water heater and a Nicholson Thermic syphon — the latter to improve the circulation of water in the boiler and accelerate the increase in pressure after lighting up and after closing the regulator. A double Kylchap exhaust and chimney were fitted. The engine retained the du Bousquet-de Glehn layout of the cylinders and the trapezoidal Belpaire firebox.

No 3566 ran her trials on 19 November 1929, almost exactly a hundred years after the triumph of Stephenson's *Rocket* at Rainhill. The results were remarkable. Chapelon's calculations were exactly fulfilled, for the engine developed about 3,000 indicated horsepower at a speed of between 75 and 80mph, hauling a heavy train and with an economy over the unrebuilt engines of 25% at normal outputs.

The long-term results were that the PO not only rebuilt many more Pacifics for its own use (including some with even further improvements), but sold some to other French railways. The Nord was so impressed with the superiority of these engines over its own crack 'Super-Pacifics' that it built some itself which were completely new — even incorporating those features which dated from 1909![6]

The next step came in 1930, though this is not a completely Pacific story. More adhesion being required on the Toulouse line, Chapelon rebuilt one of the smaller-wheeled Pacifics of the 4500 class as a 4-8-0. The existing boiler with its trapezoidal firebox, however, would not do, in the absence of a trailing truck, and a narrow firebox was needed to fit between the rear coupled wheels. Chapelon decided to use the excellent boiler of the Nord 'Super-Pacifics', but he selected the larger Belpaire firebox of Asselin's original 1914 design, which had a grate 40.4sq ft in area and was 12ft 6in long, rather than that of the 1923 engines. Like the Pacific rebuilds, the 4-8-0 had the Kylchap double exhaust and a termic siphon.

The first engine ran its trials in August 1932. The fireman had no difficulty in stoking the long narrow firebox, and Chapelon had established that this type of firebox lent itself to a higher combustion rate than that of a wide firebox of similar grate area. An additional advantage of the narrow firebox was that the automatic trimming forward of the coal tended to stop any clogging of the grate, whilst with the wide firebox the fireman had to watch every part of the grate to stop this happening.

On the first run with this rebuilt No 4521, it was apparent that the engine's performance was superior even to that of the rebuilt Pacifics. On subsequent tests the engine developed 4,000 indicated horsepower at 70mph. Eleven more engines were similarly

rebuilt and trials were carried out on the Nord, the Etat, the Est, and the PLM Railways. As a result of the PLM trials, the SNCF (which had now been formed) decided to order 25 more of these 4-8-0s for the old PLM lines. In these later rebuilds Chapelon included a number of improvements, such as an increase of 10 per cent in the volume of the low-pressure cylinders, a mechanical stoker, strengthened frames, and an enlarged boiler casing to conceal the pipework. The new engines were classified 240P and the record run of one of these engines was mentioned in the last chapter.[7]

Gresley had watched the work of Chapelon with intense interest. The trials and experience with the Kylchap exhaust, which led to its widespread adoption on the LNER, have already been mentioned, as have also his consultations with Chapelon over No 10000 and his use of wide streamlined steam passages on the A4s and P2s. The A4s, as a result, returned the best figures for coal and water consumption per drawbar horsepower hour of all the express engines tested in the locomotive exchange running of 1948. The A4, indeed, can claim to be one of the most outstanding designs in the era of British steam railway traction. It will be noted, however, that although Gresley had followed Chapelon in the design of the steam circuit, and had accepted the merits of the Kylchap exhaust, he was not convinced as to the superiority of compound over simple expansion engines. The best average figure for coal consumption per drawbar horsepower hour during the 1948 trials was 2.92 by an A4 on the Eastern Region. It will be recalled from Chapter 5 that (converting kilogrammes to pounds) a Chapelon rebuilt Pacific returned figures of 2.31 at 68mph and 2.68 at 56mph. It may be that Gresley thought the extra costs of maintenance would cancel out the superiority of the compound — though Chapelon would not agree with him on this. However, one could say that the A4 was a development of Gresley's original A1 which incorporated the lessons he had learned from Churchward and Chapelon.

In connection with the production of these remarkable A4s, J. F. Harrison writes:[8]

'It is worth recalling that from the day Gresley obtained Board authority (28 March 1935) to the start of the "Silver Jubilee" service was no more than 25 weeks, and that the first four A4s took up their duties straight out of Doncaster Works and worked for 12 months without a single locomotive failure. This building record was only achieved by the energy and drive of Robert A. Thom who was the Mechanical Engineer Doncaster. I cast the middle cylinders at Gorton and actually had to ride on the wagon to Doncaster to ensure their safe arrival.'

Cecil J. Allen rode on the train during the special run to Grantham and back behind No 2509 *Silver Link*, the first of these streamliners, on 27 September 1935, and gave a graphic and at times humorous description of this astounding run, when the engine, with a 230 ton train, ran at 100mph or over for exactly 25 miles with two peaks of 112½mph. He wrote:

'There had drifted into my compartment Sir Nigel himself, completely imperturbable, armed with a chronograph watch of vast dimensions which he had had made specially for speed recording purposes. He sat down next to me and beyond him Chas J. Brown, Chief Civil Engineer...; the latter was a nervous man, and his face betrayed the fact by being some shades paler than normally... With every fresh lurch of our coach, the Chief Mechanical Engineer directed shafts of wit at the Chief Civil Engineer concerning the condition of the latter's track, not altogether appreciated by the recipient!'[9]

As compared with the earlier Pacifics, B. Spencer states[10] that several modifications were made to ensure freer running and an ample reserve of power for uphill working. The boiler pressure was increased from 220 to 250psi, and the distance between the tube plates was reduced by just over a foot, the combustion chamber being lengthened accordingly. The piston valves were increased from 8in to 9in in diameter, and particular attention was paid to the size and shape of the steam and exhaust passages. In the actual castings the passages were carefully examined and all roughness removed. It will be perceived that, good as the A3s were, the A4s represented quite a considerable advance in design.

W. A. (or Sir William, as he later became) Stanier was a devoted disciple of G. J. Churchward, and after he became Chief Mechanical Engineer of the London Midland & Scottish Railway he frequently visited his old chief at his famous house of 'Newburn', in Swindon, for consultations. (Stanier took the name for his own home at Chorley Wood and later transferred it to his new house when he moved to Rickmansworth.) The most immediate need on the LMS was for a really powerful express locomotive which, to compete with the East Coast route, should be able to cover the 400 miles between Euston and Glasgow without a stop. This must have been one of the problems that Stanier discussed with Churchward. In the light of his own trials with *The Great Bear*, Churchward would undoubtedly have seen a Pacific as the most suitable type, and he may well have said: 'Why not take the "King" as a basis and develop it into a Pacific?' Certainly Stanier took a set of drawings of the 'King' class with him to Derby; and then, as Churchward had taken a 'Star' as the foundation on which to design his Pacific, so did Stanier derive his own Pacific from a 'King'. However, he profited by experience with *The Great Bear* to provide the radial truck with outside bearings and he added a combustion chamber, which *The Great Bear* did not have. He retained the Swindon low degree of superheat, but he had four sets of Walschaerts valve gear which he may have preferred from his experiences with the French Atlantics.

The Swindon low degree of superheat did not last long. Its success depended on perfect steaming and full pressure in the boiler, together with the excellent Welsh coal, which the Great Western used, and first class firing. If any of these conditions was not met, there was no reserve, and steam could drop to saturation point before expansion had been completed. The Stanier Pacifics did suffer from this trouble, and early in 1935 *The*

Princess Royal was fitted with a new boiler having double the superheating surface of the previous one. There was no further problem; the new boiler was excellent, and all Stanier's later engines were given high superheat.

On Monday 16 November 1936 No 6201 *Princess Elizabeth* did a very fine test run from Euston to Glasgow non-stop, returning the next day. R. A. Riddles was on the footplate and gives the following account of this remarkable run:[11]

'In the morning at Willesden I watched the coaling-up with nine tons of hand-picked coal. No 6201 was fitted with a speedometer specially for the occasion and was gone over with the proverbial tooth-comb. Similar treatment was given to No 6200 *The Princess Royal*, which was being prepared as a stand-by engine. Calculation was made of the best possible train-loading consistent with the high average speed demanded. I was to ride on the footplate and had had a continuous diagram made, on two small rollers, covering the whole of the journey. This diagram showed gradients, speed restrictions (amounting to 50, all of which had to be strictly observed) and a theoretical curve of speeds which would be needed to maintain the six-hour schedule. This apparatus was suspended from my neck in a special case, so that by turning a screw I could wind the diagram from one roller to another as the journey progressed.

'Before leaving Willesden I had impressed on the Mechanical Inspector that he must make sure that all steam pipe joints were tight in the smokebox. Judge my consternation when at 5.15pm he telephoned me to say that the left-hand main steam pipe joint had failed! This was a special stainless steel coned joint and was not available locally. It was too late to transfer all the special test fittings to No 6200. I telephoned R. C. Bond, Assistant Works Superintendent Crewe, at his home and asked him to get a spare fitting from the Works and send it to me by the driver of the 6.46pm, which was the last that day from Crewe. (The next one did not leave until after midnight.) I was extremely anxious, in fact, as to whether

Bond would be able to get the part in time, because the Works would be closed and in darkness, and the store was an immense place containing thousands of spare parts. However, Bond went straight to the house of a retired storekeeper called Frogatt who knew the place intimately and where everythng was kept. Frogatt was fortunately in and led Bond straight to the right rack, where they found the joint; and Bond was just in time to hand it to the driver of the 6.46. I met the train at Euston about 10pm, rushed the joint out to Willesden, and by 2.30am the job was done and the fire lit.

'At about 9.50am we were given the right away from Euston. The run which followed was remarkable, as extracts from the official record show. With seven vehicles weighing 225 tons tare we coverd the 401.4 miles between Euston and Glasgow in 353 minutes 38 seconds non-stop, at an average speed of 68.1mph. The maximum speed reached was 95.7mph and 83mph was sustained for 12 miles on practically level track. The ascent from Carnforth to Shap summit was a record — 31.4 miles to an altitude of 916 feet at an average speed of 70.5mph; and the 10 miles of Beattock incline were covered in 9½ minutes without the speed dropping below 56mph. Our arrival at Glasgow, 6½ minutes early, was a great thrill, and to my relief the Inspector, on going round the engine, pronounced everything in order and cold.

'We had tea at the Central Hotel in Glasgow, and the train passengers, LMS officials, and the Press were most enthusiastic over their day's experience. After tea E. J. H. Lemon, a Vice-President, got hold of me and suggested that we ought to try and run even faster on the return to London the next day. But I was opposed to trying higher speeds and suggested adding an extra coach. Lemon agreed to this.

'Later in the day we all sat down to dinner with the Scottish Directors — Chief officials of the Company, Press representatives, driver and fireman — and all seemed set for a happy celebration. Halfway through dinner I was tapped on the shoulder and told I was wanted on the telephone. A voice at the other end said; "I am sorry to tell you that my examining fitter has found all the metal out of the left-hand slide block." This was an awful blow; what on earth was I to do? We were due to leave again next day at 1.15pm and I was told that they had not even a "Scot" in good order. "Get the engine to St Rollox", I said, and start stripping down; I will be there as soon as I can." An hour later, I having been sitting without saying a word to the by now happy company, Lemon looked at me and said, "You look tired; you had better go to bed; a big day tomorrow." "Yes, sir," I said, "I would like to". And, made my escape. But what a job faced me at St Rollox! We had already experienced a lot of trouble with these crossheads, and I had arranged some months before for a centre line to be marked right round them to avoid taking out the pistons each time. This precaution saved the day; for even with this advantage it was not till 5.30am that we were coupled up again, and then had to be hauled off to the shed for firing up and preparation.

'As we were about to leave Glasgow Central on the return journey, one of our publicitymen came up and asked me to warn the driver that the film people would have very brilliant lights on the platform at Euston. I was wondering if we would even reach Beattock with a newly metalled slide block! But just an hour later we swept over Beattock summit at 66mph and, despite bad weather, went on to reach Euston 16 minutes inside the six hours, an average speed of exactly 70mph. In the two days we had run an aggregate distance of over 800 miles at a mean speed of 69mph, which was a world record for steam traction. When we got to Euston, Lemon came up to me and asked: "Riddles, why did you lose a minute to Beattock?" There was no appropriate answer!'

It was clear from this performance that Stanier had designed a very fine engine indeed, and one that was far in advance of any that had yet run on the West Coast route. Nevertheless, in the light of experience with the 'Princess' Pacifics Stanier decided that he wanted more reserve of power to operate the high-speed services which had been foreshadowed by the above trial run.

Accordingly a new Pacific was designed with a bigger boiler, larger cylinders, and coupled wheels of a greater diameter. It also had four cylinders, but the outside ones, instead of being in the Churchward position beside the rear bogie wheels, were between the bogie wheels; and instead of four sets of Walschaerts gear, the Churchward arrangement was reversed: there were two sets of Walschaerts gear with the inside valves worked by rocking shafts from the outside motion. The first batch were streamlined with single chimneys, but ultimately all the engines were unstreamlined with plain double chimneys.

On 28 June 1937 R. A. Riddles telephoned me. 'We've got a new engine at Euston!' he said, 'Would you like to come and see it?' I did, and Riddles told me that there was to be a test run to Crewe the next day but that he could not offer me a seat because every one had been allocated to railway officials or the Press. Later Riddles told me the following story of that run:[11]

'At 9.50am we set out from Euston with the new "Coronation Scot" train on its Press demonstration run. Again I was fortunate to be on the footplate, and with my diagrams laying down the postulated speeds, all was set to make an attempt on the world's maximum speed record at Whitmore, where, after a short rise, we entered on a falling gradient down to Crewe, $10\frac{1}{2}$ miles away. We had decided not to pick up water from the troughs at Whitmore, and so avoid reducing speed. The exhaust was humming with a continuous roar like that of an aeroplane engine. The white mileposts flashed past and the speedometer needle shot up through the "90s" into the "100s" to 110-111-112-113-114 miles per hour; but beyond it — no! Basford Hall sidings one and a half miles away now; spectators from Crewe coming into view at the lineside; and the train still hurtling along at 114mph. On went the brakes; off the regulator; but on we sailed with flames streaming from the tortured brake blocks. To my horror the signal was set for Platform 3 at Crewe, which has a reverse curve with a 20mph speed restriction. We were doing 60 to 70mph when we spotted the platform signal; down to 52mph through the curve, the engine riding like the great lady she is: there wasn't a thing we could do about it but hold on and let her take it. And take it she did, with the crockery smashing in the dining car: past a sea of pallid faces on the platform, till we ground to a dead stand — safe and sound and still on the rails. We had set up a new world's speed record for the steam locomotive!'

Some appalling misjudgement at Crewe had led to the train being switched to this difficult platform road. It was probably the excellent de Glehn bogie that saved the train from disaster. But all in all, it was a convincing demonstration of what a fine locomotive this was. Of course, Gresley took this record back again before long with *Mallard*, but perhaps the Kylchap exhaust had something to do with that!

The first, and streamlined, Pacific was named *Coronation*, but the first unstreamlined one, built the following year, was the *Duchess of Buccleugh*, and the whole class eventually became known as 'Duchesses'. K. R. M. Cameron has the following interesting comment on them:[12]

'So far as the LMS "Duchesses" are concerned, I would say that on the East Coast main line there would have been little to choose between them and the A1s; but they were designed for a different line with a much greater need for the higher tractive effort required for the steep gradients of Shap and Beattock. As a former LMS man one might expect me to have a preference for the "Duchess", but to be quite fair and impartial I must admit that I admired both the A1 and the A4.

Nevertheless, the "Duchess" was a beautiful engine for heavy service, if I may quote one incident which proves the point. On the occasion when flooding had cut the LMS main line from Glasgow to Carlisle, many trains came via Edinburgh (Waverley) to Carlisle by the Hawick route. The "Night Scot" sleeper on this night loaded to nearly 500 tons. At Edinburgh the "Duchess" was taken over by a St Margaret's driver who had never seen one before. I asked him if he would need bank assistance from Hawick to Whitrope, and all the comment I got was: "Which is the brake handle on this thing?" And off he went. Next day I asked him how he had managed, and was told that he did fine and had never been on a finer engine. Praise indeed from a LNE man!'

The Pacifics designed by O. V. S. Bulleid for the Southern Railway were the most controversial of all the British engines of this type. They rode well, they were fast, and they steamed well; but owing to their unconventional valve gear, they had a pretty hefty appetite for coal and water. As Cecil J. Allen says: 'Bulleid was never a man to conduct lengthy experiments with features that break away from tradition, and thus prove by a period of trial whether such features will make for increased efficiency and reliability or not.'[13] His all-welded boiler was excellent, but his chain-driven valve motion encased in an oil bath gave constant trouble.

The first of Bulleid's 'Merchant Navy' Pacifics was turned out from Eastleigh Works in 1941. The class was designed and intended for working the Dover and Folkestone boat trains and had to fit the very limited loading gauge of the old South Eastern & Chatham Railway.

The firebox was steel, selected on account of the high boiler pressure of 280psi, and there were two Nicholson thermic syphons. The boiler barrel was tapered, but on the underside instead of, as usual, at the top, so giving greater clearance for the middle cylinder, which had its valve chest above.

It is not proposed to describe these engines, or the very similar but lighter "West Country" Pacifics, in detail, because they do not contribute to the story. They were certainly an advance in power on the 'Lord Nelson' 4-6-0s, which preceded them as the Southern's leading express passenger locomotives, but they did not compare with the 'Lord Nelsons' in either reliability or economy. Bulleid's Pacifics, therefore, cannot be considered as constituting an advance in locomotive design. Bulleid tried to incorporate too many revolutionary ideas without adequate test, and trouble resulted. For instance, the chains which drove the valves stretched so that the valve gear could not be operated with precision, and the oil from the bath in which they were enclosed leaked everywhere, including the rails, so that the engines acquired an unenviable reputation for slipping. Costs for coal and maintenance were inevitably high.

In 1956 rebuilding of the Bulleid Pacifics started under the direction of R. G. Jarvis, Chief Technical Assistant at Brighton Works, as much more conventional engines with three sets of Walschaerts gear and many other modifications. All 30 of the 'Merchant Navies' were rebuilt and 60 of the 110 light Pacifics. The Jarvis re-design was a brilliant piece of work and the performance of these now very successful engines could compare with that of the Pacifics of other Regions.

We are now in a position to assess the place of the Thompson and Peppercorn Pacifics in the progressive development of this type of locomotive.

On the LMS there was a clear cut progression in the order *The Great Bear* — 'Princess' — 'Duchess', with little outside influence, except that Stanier, impressed with Chapelon's work, undertook, in conjunction with his Chief Draughtsman, a great deal of development in the size of steam passages.

The Southern Pacifics got off to a shaky start, but the rebuilds, which could really be regarded as new engines, retained the wide steam passages and thermic syphons, which probably resulted from the conversations which, on Gresley's direction, Bulleid had had with Chapelon. They also retained the Lemaître multiple jet blastpipe which Bulleid had chosen — perhaps to show his independence of Chapelon, though the latter has shown diagrammatically that it is a less efficient form that the Kylchap.[14] Bulleid's boiler was excellent, and with the vast improvement in reliability and economy effected by Jarvis, they were certainly the best express locomotives to have run on the erstwhile Southern Railway.

Gresley's Pacifics, from the original A1s to the A4s, showed a steady progress, as he adopted the best practices of other engineers and blended them with his own ideas to produce in the end a locomotive which for free steaming and running has never been surpassed — an achievement which was convincingly demonstrated when the Kylchap-fitted A4 *Mallard* broke and retained, probably for all time, the world speed record for a steam locomotive.

Much as he disliked Gresley, all the successful features of Thompson's Pacifics were inherited from Gresley. The boiler, the excellent steam circuit, and the Kylchap exhaust came from the A4. The adoption of a separate Walschaerts gear for the middle cylinder, and hence a divided drive, were necessary to meet the changed maintenance conditions. But as vehicles, all Thompson's Pacifics were notable failures. As he insisted on all connecting rods being of the same length, he had the choice between a divided drive or of all three cylinders driving on the leading coupled axle, as on Raven's Pacifics. The latter was not a good arrangement, but it was better than the one Thompson adopted. With the inevitably short connecting rods, and the resulting disposition of the outside cylinders and bogie, there arose all the troubles which have been discussed in Chapter 8. Most people who had anything to do with Thompson's Pacifics would probably have exchanged them enthusiastically for a fleet of 1908 vintage 'Great Bears', trailing truck trouble and all.

The Peppercorn Pacifics were vastly different engines. To the layman it might have appeared that the only difference from Thompson's engines was the restoration of the outside cylinders to the more usual position between the bogie wheels, but, as shown in Chapter 11, immense care was taken to build what was in effect a Gresley engine but which incorporated all those features that genius in design could suggest to improve reliability and reduce maintenance costs. The success of the Peppercorn A1s in service showed that those objects were achieved, and the last LNER Pacific design was an advance on all that had gone before. The Thompson

Pacifics, on the other hand, were much more expensive to maintain and much less reliable (in spite of the abolition of the Gresley gear) than the much older A3s and A10s. Peppercorn is unique amongst British Chief Mechanical Engineers in that the only engines for the design of which he was responsible were two classes of Pacifics.

The ancestor of all modern British two-cylinder 4-6-0 engines was No 98 of the Great Western Railway, designed by G. J. Churchward and built in March 1903. It was the most outstanding engine in Great Britain at the time of its construction, and indeed the late E. C. Poultney called it 'the keystone of the arch'[15] No 98 was the first of the line of Great Western 'Saint' class 4-6-0s, with coupled wheels of 6ft 8½in diameter. Churchward's successor Collett fitted one of these engines with wheels of the reduced diameter of 6ft, and subsequently built many more with wheels of this diameter as the 'Hall' class. Stanier took the idea with him to the LMS and produced the two-cylinder Class 5 4-6-0s (otherwise called 'Black Fives' or 'Black Staniers'), to distinguish them from the red-painted three-cylinder 'Jubilee' class). Thompson adopted the same idea in his B1 class 4-6-0 engines, and when Stanier wrote to congratulate him, he replied:

'19 Jan '43,
    My dear Stanier,
        Thank you very much for your letter of the 16th. After all, what is my new one but a Black Stanier' to LNER standards.
    How do you like the look of the ex-2-8-2 No 2005?
        Yours ever
        (Signed) Edward Thompson.

There is unfortunately no record of Stanier's reply to the question in the last sentence!

The B1 class 4-6-0 was, as already stated, an extremely good and successful engine. In the 1948 exchange trials it was in competition with a GWR 'Hall' and an LMS Class 5. (There was also a Southern 'West Country' class Pacific in the same group, but this was a much more powerful engine and not really in the same category as the other three.) Figures giving the result of these kind of trials do not necessarily mean very much, because they are affected so much by the way an engine is driven and the weather conditions prevailing at the time. However, some are perhaps worth quoting to show that the B1 had nothing to fear in comparison with the similar, but more expensively built, engines of the LMS and GWR. The average coal consumption throughout the tests in lb per drawbar horsepower hour was for the B1 3.57, the Class 5 3.54, and the 'Hall' 3.94 (though on subsequent tests with Welsh coal the 'Hall' dropped to 3.22.). The figures for water consumption in lb per dbhp-hr were B1 27.64, Class 5 27.99, and 'Hall' 29.97. (The 'West Country's' figures for coal and water respectively were 4.11 and 32.64.) The highest equivalent dbhp exerted by the B1 was 1,336, whilst climbing Wellington Bank on the Western Region at 47mph. As compared with this: the Class 5 produced 1,283 up the same bank at 50.5mph. The B1 was tackling a gradient of 1 in 175 and the Class 5 1 in 174. The 'Hall', also on this bank and with Welsh coal, managed 1,235 at 38.5mph on 1 in 90. The drawbar pull in tons of these three engines was 3.95, 3.75 and 4.5 respectively.

Cecil J. Allen remarks in his *The Locomotive Exchanges* that there was a considerable difference in the way the engines were driven. He thought that the driver of the Class 5 had as his only aim to pare his coal consumption to the very minimum, even at the expense of time, as compared with the more adventurous driving of the B1.[16]

The first British 2-8-0 freight engine was Churchward's No 97 of 1903, the prototype of his well-known and successful 28XX class which handled the Great Western heavy goods traffic until the end of the steam era. Stanier's 2-8-0s for the LMS were based on them, and when R. F. Hanks wrote to congratulate him on the splendid performance on one of these, in replacing a diesel locomotive that failed, Stanier replied with typical modesty; 'Give the credit to G. J. Churchward and the Great Western.'[17] As stated in the last chapter, R. A. Riddles's 'Austerity' 2-8-0s were related to Stanier's, and Riddles's 'Austerity' 2-10-0s were derived from the 2-8-0s. The various LNER 2-8-0s have already been discussed, and it is doubtful whether Thompson's rebuilding of the O4 as an O1 could be considered an advance on Gresley's three-cylinder O2, except on the possible saving in maintenance costs of two cylinders as compared with three.

The freight engines which were tested in the 1948 exchanges were the Stanier 8F 2-8-0, the Thompson O1 2-8-0, the Churchward 28XX 2-8-0, and the Riddles 'Austerity' 2-8-0 and 2-10-0. The average coal and water consumptions in lb per drawbar horsepower hour were respectively: O1 3.37 and 25.73, 8F 3.52 and 27.26, 28XX 3.42 and 26.80 (but with Welsh coal, 2.64 and 25.50), 'Austerity' 2-8-0 3.77 and 28.75, and 'Austerity' 2-10-0, 3.52 and 28.05. It will be noted that Churchward's 1903 engine, using its own staple diet, came in an easy first. But this did not apply only to the freight engines: the figures were the lowest of any of the engines tested. If Churchward was permitted to view the trials from a more elevated sphere, he must have indeed been gratified.

Cecil J. Allen remarks that the Austerity engines suffered from being manned by a succession of different crews, some of whom, particularly on the Western Region, had little experience of them, and he regards the excellent running results of the 2-10-0 as extremely creditable. All one need say about the O1 was that it held its own with the other engines. It seems a great pity that an O2 did not compete to show what a three-cylinder engine could do in comparison with all these two-cylinder types.

No 2-6-0s were tested in the 1948 trials, but it is safe to say that the K1 would have given a good account of herself. A large number were built under Peppercorn, and Harrison would have continued them, so that this engine obviously met a need. The rebuilt J11 was a good little engine; but it is difficult to feel that any of Thompson's other contributions to the locomotive stock are worth inclusion in this summary of achievement.

Notes

1 Andre Chapelon; *La Locomotive a Vapeur*; J. B. Bailliere et Fils, 2nd edn 1952, pp35-36
2 ibid, p37
3 A. Chapelon, letter to the author
4 F. A. S. Brown; *Nigel Gresley: Locomotive Engineer*; Ian Allan, Ltd, 1961, pp40-42
5 ibid, pp65-66
   Chapelon, op cit, p268
6 Colonel H. C. B. Rogers; *Chapelon: Genius of French Steam*; Ian Allan Ltd, 1972, pp20-30
7 ibid, pp32-37
8 J. F. Harrison, letter to the author
9 Cecil J. Allen; *British Pacific Locomotives*; Ian Allan Ltd, 1962, p56
10 B. Spencer; 'The Development of LNER Locomotive Design 1923-1941', *The Journal of the Institution of Locomotive Engineers*, vol XXXXVII (May-June 1947), pp209-210
11 Colonel H. C. B. Rogers; *The Last Steam Locomotive Engineer: R. A. Riddles, CBE*; George Allen & Unwin, 1970, pp66-69 and 86
12 K. R. M. Cameron, letter to the author
13 C. J. Allen, op cit, p156
14 Chapelon, op cit, p136
15 E. C. Poultney; *British Express Locomotive Development 1896-1948*; George Allen & Unwin, 1952), p66
16 C. J. Allen, op cit, p175

Top left: LMS Pacific No 6200 *The Princess Royal.*

Centre left: LMS Pacific No 46204 on the 10.15am Glasgow to Euston train climbing the Madeley Bank. / *Derek Cross*

Bottom left: The East Coast Pedigree: Ivatt's large boiler Atlantic No 2872 is flanked by Thompson's A2/3 Pacific No 513 *Dante* (left) and A3 No 107 *Royal Lancer* (right). / *E. R. Wethersett*

Right: All subsequent LNER Pacifics evolved from Gresley's revolutionary design of 1923, represented here by No 4480 *Enterprise* at Ganwick in 1937. / *E. R. Wethersett*

Below: The A4s constituted a major advance in design, particularly in respect of the design of steam and exhaust passages, and made still more effective by the fitting of Kylchap blastpipes and double chimneys. Top Shed's No 60034 *Lord Faringdon* heads past Woolmer Green in 1959. / *E. R. Wethersett*

Top left: LMS 'Duchess' class Pacific No 46232 *Duchess of Montrose* in Crewe Works Yard, 15 March 1959. / *K. R. Pirt*

Centre left: LMS 'Duchess' class Pacific No 46256 *Sir William A. Stanier FRS*, 2 August 1958. / *J. B. Bucknall*

Bottom left: A striking shot of A1 No 60155 *Borderer* as it prepares to turn on to the down fast line just north of York with an unfitted freight — by 1965 the A1s were relegated to menial jobs. / *J. B. Benson*

Right: A1 No 60157 makes for Gateshead shed after arrival at Newcastle Central. / *I. S. Carr*

Below: Towards the end of their lives the A2s were used between Glasgow and Aberdeen. No 60527 *Sun Chariot* accelerates away from Hilton Junction, Perth, with the up 'Grampian' July 1963. / *Eric Oldham*

Bottom: Thompson A2/3 No 60521 *Watling Street* leaves York with a down express in April 1956. / *P. Ransome-Wallis*

Right: The B1 was an 'extremely good and successful engine'. No 1219 was photographed near Ryton on the Carlisle-Newcastle line with an up stopping train. / *E. R. Wethersett*

Below: Gresley and Thompson in harness as preserved B1 No 1306 double-heads *Flying Scotsman* over the Furness line on a special returning to Carnforth in 1976. / *R. E. B. Siviter*

Bottom: The K1s met a useful need up to the end of steam such as No 62041 on a Ferryhill to West Hartlepool dolomite train in 1966. / *J. M. Boyes*

Index